the

Daily Insight

Companion

A step by step guide
to health, healing & happiness

by Tracey McBeath

The Health & Healing Coach

TRACEY MCBEATH

The Health & Healing Coach.

tracey@traceymcbeath.com.au

www.traceymcbeath.com.au

Dear Reader,

This book is a very special book. It was created over 6 months for members in my long-term group program, The Art of Thriving. Every morning, I got up early to show them how we must show up for ourselves, every single day. I shared an insight designed to help them see this path within themselves. It is this that is now this book for you.

Showing up for yourself every day, to choose what you want to choose for yourself, is a habit. We have to cultivate this every day in order to gain the clarity we need around the choices we have.

We mostly run our lives from our subconscious mind. That automatic pilot is deciding for us based on our past choices, our beliefs, and experiences. It's about staying where you are and choosing the path you've already taken. It's not about carving out a new one.

With the daily practice of being willing to look somewhere new, we will be gifted with the insight to see something new. To create the life we want through awareness of the choices we are making in how we treat ourselves, and others, every single day.

How to read this book?

I encourage you to reflect on one insight every day. Don't read it looking to confirm what you think you already know. Show up with an open and curious mind and see what is presented to you. Open your heart, open your mind to what is possible.

We are always being presented with choices in every single day of our lives. Always. Without exception.

Our job is to give ourselves the gift of the insights needed to see choice, where we may currently not see that we have any. If the choices we are making are hurting ourselves or others, we can choose another path.

To do so, we need to be willing to look in a different direction, sit with what comes up, then make a different choice to the one our minds want us to make.

I hope with this book as your companion, you can learn to follow your heart. Which always knows the best way forward for us.

We only need to tune in to it and listen.

Much Love,

Tracey xxx

The Daily Insight

"Let go of the battle. Breathe quietly and let it be. Let your body relax and your heart soften." Jack Kornfield.

Simple Breath Work

Breath work during the day.

Breathing in through the nose for 5 seconds, hold for 5 seconds, breathing out for 5 seconds, then hold for 5 seconds.

Repeat at least 4 times.

That's one session, try to do 4 sessions each day.

Reminder app (I use Nudge)

Notice – your mind, your body, your being.

Sometimes, often the simplest things we can do are the most helpful. Our mind loves to complicate things. It keeps itself busy, but often at the same time innocently makes it harder for you to see the simple things you can do.

When we have a nervous system that is dysregulated due to high levels of stress over long periods of time, we don't breathe optimally. We tend to shallow breath into our

chest (instead of our abdomen). The risks to our health over time from this are high.

So, if all you start to do today is to incorporate this breathing routine into your everyday life, what might change for you? The key is you will have to remind yourself through an app to do it regularly. Your conscious mind will easily forget until it becomes a habit.

the Daily Insight

Why could journaling help?

I think it's important to see that something like journaling may help you see beyond the habits that look like they're keeping you stuck. Allowing you to observe more closely what choices/reactions are made each day on auto pilot - which we know is where we can easily get stuck. A journal can become a safe place to share with your heart, stretch your mind, make commitments to yourself, and just simply be yourself. No judgement.

But if it's not for you, that's ok.

There's no 'must do' to achieve your health and healing goals. There are many ways we can create the space for insight, which is essential for change. But... remember our **W** from our **OWL**? Willingness. Could you be willing to suspend the belief that it isn't for you? See what happens if you give it a go, even if your mind is full of stories otherwise!

Could you commit to just 1 or 2 minutes each day to write what you notice?

Make this small commitment to yourself. Not big...small. Not as another 'task' you must do (there's no joy in that), but as something you are

willing to do to see where it takes you. As something that you can do no matter what else goes on in your day. To become a comfort, a way to notice, to practice doing... even if there is mental resistance to doing it.

Be the witness to your life. Allow the journal in your inner world.

Start there and see where it takes you. Making them small (please keep them small!) daily commitments to yourself are super important in re-building that trust in you.

Remember we can either keep doing things in the same way, getting the same results... or we step into the discomfort of growth and try new things.

Have you got a good visual picture of where you want to be? How your future self might behave in certain situations, especially in areas where you feel your reactions and choices are not helping you? This is something worth writing about in your journal.

How do you want to treat yourself and others in the world? What do you value? See where you want to be... and move your thoughts towards that.

The mind is so much more powerful than we can ever possibly imagine.

Our minds and body are intricately connected. What we think, our body hears and feels. We always live in the feeling of our thinking, and through our vagus nerve, our whole body hears it.

You've all heard of the placebo effect? This proves that the mind can change the body in positive and powerful ways. But have you heard about the nocebo effect? This occurs when our thoughts make us worse... not better. Both have been seen in research - a man was told he had cancer and died 6 weeks later. The only issue is he didn't have cancer, it was a mistaken diagnosis. Athletes have been injected with a

super serum to make them perform faster... they all perform better, yet the serum is just saline.

One of the biggest powers we all have that is very underutilised is the belief we can change. We can heal.

In fact, we must believe it if we want it to happen. Where you start is here.

So, what do you believe? Ask yourself this question and be honest with your answers. Challenge everything. Use your superpowers of your mind to work for you... not against you any longer. The underutilised power that is available to you is enormous.

The Daily Insight

Looking for Patterns

Patterns are far easier to notice than isolated events or responses. Patterns let you know that you are responding less to whatever is going on outside yourself and more to your own habits and assumptions.

What do you most commonly tell yourself when you get up in the morning? What do you expect when you open your emails?

How do you react when someone asks you to do something you don't feel like doing - or they criticise you?

Are you constantly defending your own actions in your own mind? Are you surprised when things go well?

How do you react when you're angry, sad, stressed, or tired?

Recognising your patterns helps bring what is subconscious and automatic to our conscious awareness. It takes away its power and helps you to see choice.

Use your journal to write down what you notice. What patterns did I observe today? Don't be afraid to look. It's not about having to do 'more'

work. It's about shining a light on your experience so you can be more in control of your reaction to it.

the Daily Insight

Just like peaceful reflections at the beginning of the day set your intentions, reflections at the end of the day can be powerful as well.

Spending a couple of minutes at the end of each day asking yourself... What did I learn today? What surprised me?

You can use one or two of these practical prompts to guide you in your awareness.

Observe your impact on others.

Listen carefully to your internal stories.

Know what your strengths are.

Find out what matters to you.

Notice what brings you joy.

Notice what has a negative effect on your moods.

Experience how much you can learn from your mistakes.

Learn from other people.

Get to know the contents of your inner world (your dreams, hopes, wishes, what you dwell on, how you interpret situations).

Assume there is always more to know.

The **OWL**. She is like you. Wise, strong, and can see in many directions.

The **O** in **OWL**, is where we start. In the observations. Noticing, observing.

As an adult, we often speed through life without much observation of our patterns, reactions, inner world, expectations, judgements, choices. And who are we responsible for all of this.

Without observation, we can't start to make a different choice.

This is particularly relevant when it comes to patterns in our life that hurt us (or others) whether that is physical, emotional, short- or long-term damage.

There isn't much we need to do when it comes to Observation. We only need to slow down, and look. Sounds easy, but for most of us, it's not.

Most of us never consciously slow down for fear of what we might see. What if we see something we don't like? What if there is more 'work' for me to do? What if I experience uncomfortable feelings? What then? What would I do? What if I

get bored? Imagine if I got bored and didn't have anything to do....

None of that is likely to be conscious thought.

But your body knows it all. You are just not tuned in to it. None of us really are. But we continue to ignore it at our own risk.

Change requires you to show up to yourself, and to your life, every single day.

Actually, I would say to live a life aligned with your values - your heart - it requires you to consciously show up for yourself every single day you're gifted with being here on earth.

And when we start to do this, we will gain clarity on the patterns in our life that are hurting us and keeping us psychologically stuck.

So, pick up some compassion, some kindness, some courage. Take it all with you as you start to **OBSERVE**.

Witness it without judgement.

Share with someone, share with us, share it privately in your journal. But look. No more pretending we can't see.

Then get curious as to how it may feel to change that pattern in your life. Curiosity is a value that is a true gift to access in this life.

14

The Daily Insight

One simple truth that changed my life.

I am not my thoughts; I am not my moods. Thoughts come - both positive and negative ones - and they go. I don't have to believe or grab any of them or give them space in my head or heart.

This is applicable to ALL thoughts. The I am too tired thought, the I can't be bothered thought, the I'm not good enough thought, the I may as well eat the whole packet now thought, the I'm not confident enough thought, the I can't change thought...

All thought. And not just the ones we notice.

Thought is what drives our behaviour. Behaviour creates our life. But when we only get busy changing our behaviour, without understanding that thought is driving it, we rarely are successful at change beyond our willpower.

This truth can be hard to recognise because of several reasons. Firstly, 95% of all we do comes from unconscious thought, much of which has been buried from childhood experiences. We are totally unaware of the thinking driving our behaviour, and if that's the case, totally unable

to change the behaviour until we become aware of the thinking behind it. Not to analyse... but to simply notice that it's no longer worthy of your attention because it's taking you away from the life you want to have.

This noticing requires courage to do, and most won't ever do it. But you will because we will do this together. And you will see as you look in this direction that the fear is made up thought.

Conscious awareness of our thinking brings choice. Without a feeling of consciously choosing our behaviour, we are not free to live our own life.

the Daily Insight

I think this may be one of the most important insights for you to hear. And I mean hear, deeply.

It is long.

I hope this gives you hope and helps you shed any shame you're carrying that has you falsely believe you can't change and heal. This post follows on from yesterdays.

Becoming 'conscious' enough to be able to witness our internal world is fundamental to any change that is to be successful beyond the short term.

It's consciousness that makes us human. Yet most of us are so immersed in our inner world - so 'unconscious' that we are not aware there is a script continually running through our minds.

We believe the script is 'us'. But it is not us - it is our thoughts, and we just happen to practise them all day long.

You are the thinker of your thoughts, not the thoughts themselves. Thoughts are electrochemical responses that happen thanks to the firing of neurons in the brain. Thoughts serve a purpose - they allow us to problem solve, create, form connections.

But when we rely too much on them as most of us do, there is no space to breathe and examine them.

When we're trapped in a state of reactivity, clarity is virtually impossible. So is listening to our intuition - a very real concept that refers to our innate wisdom. Our gut feeling, sixth sense, heart brain. I've talked about this many times before. It's never gone... only ever buried.

Now I truly see why for some of us it's so difficult, if not impossible, to reconnect back to it.It's only when you are conscious that you can really 'see' yourself. All those hidden forces that are at work manipulating, moulding and holding you back.

I have deeply seen recently that you can't change your lifestyle long term, stop drinking, eat better, or improve yourself in any way until you become more transparent to yourself.

If you truly know what to do to improve your health and your life, like I know most of you do, why don't you do it? Because you just haven't seen what you need to see yet.

It's NOT a moral failure; it's because you're stuck repeating those behaviours that are now essentially automatic behaviours.

Witnessing can be hard to do when our nervous system is dysregulated. Our responses become like breathing. Automatic and autopilot.

This is why an inability to make change stick isn't your fault. If you're stuck with shame and guilt that you 'can't change' it will be holding you back. And I want to release you from that.

Because it is a release when you finally accept this truth.

A dysregulated nervous system – cyclical thoughts, behaviours, emotional explosions, detachments – have a physiological basis: they are the negative impulses of a dysregulated body.

You are not bad or damaged.

In fact, these behaviours are learned responses that your body uses to keep you alive. Like breathing, they are survival mechanisms.The great news is that while so much may seem out of your conscious control, you are not at the whim of your body. Just because you may have a dysregulated nervous system – like I did and still do to some extent (it's a lifelong healing process) – you can change.

If your body could learn dysregulated ways of coping, it can also learn healthy ways to recover.

As Dr Nicole LePera tells us, epigenetics shows us genes are not fixed. Neuroplasticity shows us the brain can form new pathways. The conscious mind has shown us the power of our thoughts to change. Polyvagal theory has shown us that the nervous system affects all other systems of the body.

And when you start to shed layer after layer of misunderstandings and ignorance about the connections of the mind, body, and soul, and start to really witness yourself (not just pretend to do it... actually do it), you will begin to comprehend your potential to heal.

We CAN unlearn and relearn as adults.

Start the process of witnessing. But you may not notice the thought. Instead, I want you to notice your body, which is reflecting your thoughts.

Notice your body. The sensations, the feelings, what it is saying to you. Use your journal to write it all down.

Don't judge it... observe it.

Write a reminder on your phone to spend a few minutes every day to notice. Where is your focus? On autopilot? What can you see? What can you hear? What can you feel in your body?

The Daily Insight

The inner critic is just your subconscious mind trying to control you. It is a gift to know it is a normal act of the subconscious mind only trying to protect me. I have learnt to watch it all, sometimes laugh, allow it to be as it is, then let it all go.

This is noticing. This is witnessing. Not being hooked in by it and have your body shoot off a stress response that my whole body would feel... and be affected by. It's not about having the thoughts there.

Did you know our stress response (which is triggered by a fearful thought) is only supposed to last 90 seconds? That's how long it takes to do the loop through our body and for our nervous system to have the ability to return to normal. But when we get stuck in thinking loops, it can remain on for hours/days at a time, totally wreaking havoc on all parts of our body and mind. It's a vital part to healing most don't understand.

So back to noticing. This is your hardest job to do, but the one that will give you freedom through choice.

Can you notice today when your subconscious is wanting to run the show? Can you feel what

your body is saying? Where are you and what are you doing?

Know it's just trying to protect you. But it's what is keeping you stuck. And without noticing, you can't leave it behind.

It's not about never having these thoughts, or these responses being triggered. It's a goal that will see you burn out with exhaustion and get nowhere. It's about learning to watch them from a distance. To allow them to come up... then to go. Without them dragging you in. There is nothing in there for you. As loud as it might be demanding there is.

What can you do to step back and calm your nervous system when you do start to notice?

Ground yourself to the present moment. Be present to the task at hand in front of you. Breathe deeply. Go outside. Journal.

In fact, don't wait for this to happen to practise being in the present moment.

Doing it regularly throughout the day when you're feeling fine is a great way to build the awareness to do it when you really need it. And you will be improving your nervous system flexibility in the process.

the Daily Insight

Challenging that subconscious mind requires insights at many levels. Today I want to share a simple tool that has helped many really see how much it runs the show, and to take a little conscious choice back from it.

Introducing the considering cup. If this isn't new to you, maybe you've forgotten it's there to help you. So here it is.

As part of your witnessing and noticing this week (and always), start to watch with curiosity just how quickly your mind wants to dismiss new ideas. You will see it when you look.

You react instantly when you don't notice it. "Oh that's ridiculous."

"I can never do that."

"I can't change." "You're wrong." "You're stupid." Etc.

But it's what happens too when we make those choices that are damaging our health. Our mind craves, we react, without pause for reflection and consciously choosing whether we want to listen to the cravings of the mind or not.

So, how can this cup help?

Now it is a metaphor, but many have used a real cup.

When you notice your mind wanting to act by instantly dismissing a new idea, or hooking you into your health damaging behaviours, stop and put it in your considering cup. Write it down on a bit of paper if you like (it helps more) and pop it in there. Leave it there for a bit. How long will depend on what it is. Could be minutes to days.

Doing this will automatically create that essential space to tap into your heart's values and see if there is indeed something in there for you to consider.

Increasing your awareness that you have a choice in everything you do is what you're aiming for.

Without this, our subconscious mind will continue to run the show. Choice is what we all have, we just can't all see it... until we do.

The Daily Insight

Calming the inner chatter.

However chaotic, overwhelming, or disappointing your life may feel at any given moment, your deepest nature beyond that noisy part of your brain is still, silent, and stable.

There are many ways to begin to experience that stillness, to quieten your inner chatter that is totally focused on the past or future and develop your connection with that part of your brain that connects to your heart.

Meditation, prayer, inspirational reading, being in nature, mindfulness, calling up an image of stillness to counteract the noise, focusing on qualities and values, creating positive intentions, writing a letter to your inner wisdom are just some.

There is a meditation that I use sometimes when my mind is noisy and loud, and I want to calm it. Know that it is this incessant internal chatter that is what is exhausting.

Especially when we're innocently negotiating with it all.

Stepping away from the internal chatter and into the present moment is our path to peace

of mind (but remember your subconscious mind won't agree with that).

"Imagine a blue/green ocean, with sand swirling through the water. As the sand settles to the bottom of the ocean floor, I imagine my 'busy' thoughts also settling, lying down, taking a rest and giving me the rest, I need. As my thoughts settle, I let my awareness expand. Continuing to watch the water imaginatively, I see how calm it has become.

Then, as the water becomes completely still, sunlight strikes it and the water itself becomes infinitely light."

The Daily Insight

How to comfort yourself... that is not food.

We've all learned coping behaviours that align with food. We learned to eat when we were sad, hurt, bored or in any way uncomfortable. Over time, this became the subconscious response when we were sitting in an uncomfortable emotion, which we have to start to notice in order to challenge it.

Relearning new ways to comfort yourself when you feel pushed around by your moods and emotions is an essential part of healing.

Learning new ways to comfort yourself dramatically increases self-trust. It also lets you know that whatever arises, you can deal with it.

But you can't deal with anything you keep running away from or you can't even see.

New self-soothing skills can be easily learned, but like anything new, they must be practised. And of course, you will be coming up against your mighty subconscious mind, so it will require you to become present and conscious.

When you learn these new skills, you will be helping to build a resilient nervous system. You will help your body to switch off the

fight/fight/freeze response that creates all the discomfort within your body.

It will bring you to an increased level of awareness and help you in your quest to be a witness to your thoughts, thus coping with it all far more effectively (and no need to reach for the food).

Trust yourself that switching to soothe is possible. Here's how.

Recognise the symptoms of panic, anxiety, or mounting fear. You will feel them in your body as I've said repeatedly. Know you're capable of switching to soothe. Become aware of what your subconscious mind wants you to do (hint: it will be a very familiar pattern to you when you look).

Tell yourself as often as you can, 'I CAN deal with this.' This powerful message will affect you physically and emotionally. It doesn't matter that you don't know how to deal with it; what matters is that you will.

While you're telling yourself 'I can deal with this,' you are not able to stay in that loop of how awful it is, how hopeless you are, how frightful and disappointing life is.

Write down what the issue is (another gold for your journal). Putting it 'out there' on a piece of paper makes space in your mind. It also gives

you a little distance. Use as few words as possible to describe it.

Ask yourself, "does this need my attention now?" Often when we're in a panic, you are the least creative or effective. If the matter isn't urgent, switch your attention to something else (that beautiful meditation from yesterday, a walk, the noticing mindfulness exercise, yoga, etc.).

Your mind can only think about one thing at a time. Switch your mind from victim to problem solver. Sit up straight, breathe deeply, shoulders back. Your mind will immediately benefit.

Learn not to trust your decision making in these times. Your thinking will be distorted and so will your reactions. Take your time. Focus on calming yourself first, and only then on dealing with the issue or problem.

Sometimes you need to get some physical distance from what's worrying you. You won't take the problem with you if you tell yourself that you're in the process of dealing with it.

Do something that is physically demanding. Digging your garden, walking briskly, swimming... what the activity is will be less important than acting, changing your environment, and with that, your thoughts, and feelings.

If your mind keeps taking you back (I'm sure it will) to the issue, just repeat the same steps. "I

can deal with this"; writing down the problem; switching your attention; doing something physically demanding. Also remind yourself that clarity isn't found in the weeds. It comes when it clears. Get bored with this process. It will help you.

When things have cleared up and you're feeling calmer, look at what you've written down. Do you see the problem or issue differently now? If so, write down what you see.

Now ask yourself, who is the wisest, cleverest, and kindest person I know? (You don't have to know them personally). Once you have identified this person, ask yourself. "How would they deal with this?"

Do not underestimate the power of your own imagination. It is your thoughts themselves that have produced those powerful systems of stress or anxiety. Harness that same imaginative power now to support you and see what needs to be done - if anything.

Write down what you imagine their answer would be. The insights you are looking for will be helpful, kind, supportive and manageable.

Know that some problems are not going to be solved; they will only be outlived. Recognising the truth of that can also be surprisingly soothing.

Notice as often as you can just how severe a problem looks and feels when you are hungry, exhausted, overwhelmed or stressed.

It's the perfect storm for your subconscious mind to take over. Use your panic as the wisdom it is - an invaluable alarm bell on your dashboard wanting you to pay more attention to your life.

Ask yourself: what extra stress is happening right now in my life? What would help me deal with this stress?

Who could I talk to about this?

How have I got through this kind of tough time before?

Remind yourself that whatever is happening is not all of who you are; nor is it how things will always be.

You can deal with this.

How we work: it's simple, yet we make it so complicated!

We cannot work in any other way. The cravings (urges) don't always last, hence the brackets.

Sometimes when we start 'The work', we've got no awareness of any of it. Many I talk about this to have never given it any thought.

If we want to change our behaviour, we must know where it comes from, and take responsibility for it. No one is responsible for the way you act, except for you.

Some people start by noticing the thoughts. Some notice the feeling. But without noticing either of those, we don't get to build in choice before the action.

It can also work the other way around. Change behaviour by doing what is healing (regardless of the thoughts or feelings), then notice what comes after.

For example: choose nutrient dense eggs and meat, what happens to your thoughts and feelings? Choose sugar and processed junk, what happens then?

If you have the habit of ignoring your values over the weekend, see if you can keep them with you. Notice the thoughts, cravings (urges), feelings, but you get to decide.

Your body's wisdom knows what you need. Listen to it. Not the cravings of the mind.

"Your beliefs become your thoughts
Your thoughts become your words
Your words become your actions
Your actions become your habits
Your habits become your values
Your values become your destiny."
Bruce Lipton PhD.

The Daily Insight

Almost all of us spend significant chunks of our lives worrying that others will find us 'too' something: too old, too young, too rich, too poor, too much, too fat, too thin, too quiet.

Or maybe we worry that others might see us as 'not enough': not smart enough, young enough, original enough, pretty enough, successful enough, important enough...

We credit those judgments to other people. Just as likely though, those are the harsh thoughts and judgments growing like weeds in our own minds.

And those thoughts are not loving - or helpful.

You give enormous power away when this kind of too much/too little attitude has you in its grip. And you seriously undermine your relationships with other people.

It's hard to feel good about someone when you're telling yourself that they are judging you, you push them away or disbelieve them. This, too, damages your relationships.

In this kind of situation, you are giving power not to what other people think about you. Instead, you are giving power to the thoughts

you assume they are having about you (which you honestly can never truly know).

Those assumptions are convincing because they coincide with your own worst fears. In fact, they are your own worst fears! You are attributing those views to someone else - but it's you who is driving them.

When judgmental thoughts persist, take a reality check. Give others - and yourself - the benefit of the doubt.

Recognise that the judgements originate in your mind - and that you are attributing them to other people.

Know that you will read 'cues' negatively when you feel anxious or self-doubting (watch how much you notice this when you look)

Accept you are not always uppermost in other people's thoughts. Most people are thinking about themselves, rather than you (and perhaps, fearing your judgements)

Ask yourself whether there's a pattern to this kind of thinking: both a pattern in the judgements themselves and when they occur (timing, who with etc.)

You might even want to check with someone close to you, "Am I often talking about how badly done by I am or how misjudged I feel?"

Most of us are highly sensitive about certain issues and this may get even worse at times. Once you get a handle on that, it's much easier to see how your own attitudes (and fears) drive your interpretations of other people's behaviour.

Check if your 'worst fears' arise from a guilty conscience. Is there something they really need changing, doing, addressing? If so, take the assumed judgement as a useful signal. It can be a useful catalyst for change if you're honest with yourself.

Accept that you will be 'too-something' for some people at least some of the time. This says more about them than you (usually). You will deal with it most easily when your opinion of yourself doesn't rest on what you assume other people are thinking.

The ultimate gift?

I was well into adulthood (I mean... only 5 years or so ago!) before I 'got it' that this life of mine was an incredible gift. I was thinking this morning while enjoying my own company on a 3 hour walk that for so much of my life, I was so preoccupied with what was 'wrong' with me... instead of appreciating things as they are.

I always fell short of whatever vision of perfection I had created in my mind, and I believed that what was wrong with me required far more of my attention than what was 'right'.

A few things happened that challenged my thought systems on this. Firstly, I came to see how finite this life is.

I started to come each day to see it as a gift, not for what I could 'do' with it, but for what it was. Many people express the view they it is not until they know they are dying that they live fully and truthfully focusing on what's important and discarding what's not.

But the reality is, we're all dying. Our death may be days away; it may be decades away. But there is no avoiding it.

Understanding how very precious life is, and seeing how fiercely and tenderly people cling to life when they know how little time they have left, I also realised that like any love, our love for life soars when we allow it to be unconditional.

What this means to me is loving life even when it's not following my orders, wishes or desires; loving life even when it feels massively unfair, unsafe, disappointing, or tragic... loving life even when I am not getting what I want from it.

I don't think most of us realise, unless we are fortunate enough to be dying consciously, how conditional our love affair with life really is; how much we complain and how offended we feel when we don't get what life 'owes' to us.

Unconditional love for life means (well to me), entering life fully. Taking it all on. Saying 'yes' to everything: to the suffering and the compassion; to the ignorance and the wisdom; to the brutality as well as the radiance and beauty; to the disappointments and the triumphs.

Of course, I welcome some things more easily than others; of course, I am concerned with keeping myself safe; of course I want to do my bit for kindness and goodness and beauty. But loving life only if or when it gives me what I want would keep me from being real.

Buddha teaches that:

This gift of life is precious. My gift of life is intrinsically precious (so is yours)

Human existence is precious.

The chance to reflect upon the big questions is precious.

Every life offers a constant repertoire of opportunities to become more at peace and wiser. Taking up those opportunities is precious.

For most of my life, these insights were buried under deeply conditioned thought that taught ideas about sin, guilt, unworthiness, insufficiency ... that carried deep psychological power to wound and damage (as we saw last night).

Our deep sense of being 'wrong' or unworthy of love, our distrust of our own strengths, our ability to hurt ourselves and others, are all born from a lack of awareness and trust that our lives are precious: that life itself is infinitely precious. And when I get caught up in my mind and day to day living and forget these truths? I now don't beat myself up for my shortcomings or blame myself.

I just need to remember.

the Daily Insight

Our beliefs are heard by every cell in our body. Our cells don't just respond to what we eat. They also respond to what we think and believe.

Addressing our subconscious beliefs is so important. And that starts with understanding we all have them, we're mostly unaware of them, and they're usually self-limiting and disempowering.

But if we can learn those beliefs, we can learn new ones that are empowering and limitless.

Healing is about creating the space for choice where you currently can't see that you have choice. Insight helps you to become aware of the thoughts and feelings behind your choices.

And for the behaviours you do in which you don't feel like you have a choice, these will help you see that you indeed, do.

How do we do this?

While there are many paths that lead us back home, let me share with you what has been the most powerful for me. Every morning, when I wake up, I remind myself that I indeed have access to choose. Choices in how to react to anything that comes into my day.

I remember this quiet courage that lives within me - and by the way, this lives within you as well. It is never gone; it's waiting patiently for you to connect to it. It is with this awareness that I get to consciously choose go down a path that reflects my values with how I treat myself and others around me. That I get to input the coordinates into my inner GPS that will take me down my path of living an authentic life... without regrets.

The path I know will mean that I am the navigator of my own life.

The Daily Insight

My reflections today came from probably my favourite writer, Yung Pueblo. I love his writing. They speak directly to my own healing, and he writes in ways I can only aspire to. Today, on my wedding anniversary, it seems fitting to share some thoughts on love. And how it all starts with the love you have for yourself.

I have only discovered that for myself over the last 10 years. I finally stopped running away from myself and saw that nothing I changed outside of myself would make a scrap of difference until I did the work within. The journey within is the best one you will ever go on.

"The biggest shift in life happens when you go inward.

You step in and observe all that you find with acceptance; The love you bring lights up your self-awareness.

You start seeing how the past is packed into your mind and heart - Patience, honesty, and observation start the healing process.

With time, intention, and good healing practices, the past loses its power over your life.

You continue the process - stepping in, feeling, understanding, and letting go. And then you

start noticing the results; you are not the same anymore.

Your mind feels lighter and develops a new, sharper clarity.

You start arriving at your life and relationships ready for deeper connection."

The love for yourself opens up a world where love is limitless. You can feel love for anyone you meet when you connect with them beyond their habitual minds. My life and work is so rich because I see you. I see who you truly are beyond your deep conditioned thinking. My job is simply to give you the healing practices needed to allow you to see yourself from this place as well.

Love is the answer to all that you seek. And it lives in abundance within you.

The Daily Insight

Just a point on feeling behind.

We're never behind in life. We can only ever be here.

The behind thoughts are just your mind trying to navigate it all and trying to make sense of things.

You don't have to pay attention to it - notice it, let it be there, then refocus on today.

When we focus on the thoughts that make us feel like we're behind, we miss the moments and opportunities that are there for us today.

That beautiful regift of every morning... or, the gift of any moment to refocus our attention to the present moment.

The Daily Insight

Today I want to share a little bit on how to reflect. Experiences in and of themselves are valuable, and they create your life. But they become even more valuable when you know how to reflect on them, learn, then move on. Reflecting isn't ruminating, which many of us are so good at doing. Ruminating looks like endlessly going over and over the same ground without gaining insight or relief.

Reflecting means focusing, daring to go a little deeper than usual, looking at the situation with curiosity, interest, and a bit of distance. Sometimes it's achieved in a few moments of quiet thought; sometimes in a conversation with a trusted friend, a loved one. Your journal can also be a teacher here, letting you reflect in your own way and at your own pace.

These questions may help:

> ➢ What's familiar here? (Is this a pattern? Pattern recognition is what we are starting to notice)

> ➢ What were my intentions in this situation? What was I hoping for or wanting?

> ➢ What happened?

- ➢ How might this have looked from the perspective of whoever else was involved?

- ➢ What can I see now that I didn't then?

- ➢ What would I do more of – or less of – another time?

Write down in your journal whatever insight you have gained, no matter how small. Then literally 'close the book' on it. And awaken to a fresh new moment. Remember that a journal or notebook entry can be just a few lines – yet still be fresh and invaluable in freeing you to get back to your day. If you find it hard, that's ok. Don't make it worse for yourself by making it yet another thing you find hard to do. Just let it be as it is and continue to do the work to calm your body.

Breathe, step outside, or just write in your journal with no judgement or restriction.

the Daily Insight

Chatting with my 19-year-old daughter today about an upcoming talk I'm giving to two groups of VCE students. I was running through a few thoughts I had, and I asked her what she thought. She started saying a few things (we were in the car - the best place to chat with your kids), and they were so insightful, I asked her to write them down in my notes.

I thought you might enjoy these insights as well. Here's what Tara wrote:

"Tara genius ideas

It's okay to do nothing.

Think of sleep and winding down as a positive thing that you do for you. Not another thing you 'have' to do.

You're ok, even when you feel like you're not ok. Humans feel stuff. We don't feel good all the time. The bad days must come. Leave them alone and they will go on their own. Have a teacher, friend, or your mum to talk to when you need to talk to someone or if you feel sad.

Don't trust your thoughts when you don't feel good. They're lying to you! They trick you into believing you're not good enough! It's not true! Don't listen to them when they're saying those

things. Do something fun or go hang out with your friends instead of listening to what they are saying about you. Your thoughts are not you. You don't need to believe them."

I think she would be much better giving this talk than me!

Reminded me of one of my favourite quotes by Dr Wayne Dyer, "when you change the way you look at things, the things you look at change."

The Daily Insight

Old fears, new feelings. Do our fears ever really leave us, or do we have to live around them forever? How do we move through our fears from the past into a more courageous, open approach to life?

I wonder if you can get curious and start to experiment with looking at fear itself more compassionately. The fears we feel during tough times in life are a legitimate response to difficult situations. What else should we feel during those times?

Our brains are so well designed to look after us that they can start to point us towards fear, when there really are only shadows. Our automatic response to things becomes fearful. But we can learn to notice when we're looking at past shadows and when we're not.

When we are deep inside a difficult situation, it's quite natural that we would wish it away. And after it's over we probably will wish it never happened. But we can learn more about life, and who we are if we let these times be our teachers. The person who has not been afraid has had no reason to seek and find courage.

Do our fears ever really leave us? I would say that we can learn to react less to them - to be

less afraid of fear, which we can do when we meet it with love.

Sometimes fear is our friend: it can be a warning of what is dangerous ahead, and we need to trust ourselves to listen when it's truly needed.

But when it's not the case, and we start to see that our fear lies more within us than outside us, we can learn to ask, what is fear teaching me here? Where is it taking me?

If I look deeply in its face - if I look at fear fearlessly - what will it become?

Any situation met with love changes its shape. I notice my shadow fears and thank them for trying to look after me. But they are no longer the ones who are writing my show. We can learn to ask what the situation needs, whether we are afraid or not.

Responding then to the moment... not our emotions.

The Daily Insight

Today I'm sharing from my book, insight 35, You Have Today.

When I feel lost or unsure of where I'm going, I like to remind myself of the things I know. There is so much I don't know. But remembering what I do reminds me that I'm human.

And so is everyone else around me.

We're all doing the best we can at the level of awareness we're sitting at. When awareness increases, so do our choices.

Everything passes.

Feelings are created within me. I don't have to judge them or will them away, they will leave when my thinking changes (which it will, like the weather will).

We only have the present moment.

I am free to express my own opinions, and so is everyone else.

I don't need anyone else to agree with me, to validate my own view.

My view is a product of my own thought system which means it will be limited by what I've seen,

heard, experienced and believe. So is everyone else's. This makes it my reality, but not reality.

Change happens when we transcend our beliefs and look to learn beyond them.

If my opinion differs from yours, it's not about you. It's not personal. It doesn't make you wrong, it doesn't make me right. It is just that way because of the way humans work.

We can choose to be offended... or curious.

This isn't a dress rehearsal.

The journey is in the experience. Joy lives there too.

I operate either from love or fear. Fear is limited and a mental prison. Love is limitless and creates freedom. I always have a choice.

My first reaction to my thinking is not usually my best. Creating space between the thought and the reaction gives me more choice.

I am enough now.

When I feel the urge to change my external environment, it's my wisdom telling me to look within.

I may not agree with and like what others say, but I respect their right to say it.

The Daily Insight

What does showing up for yourself mean?

It simply means to make a commitment to become aware. To notice your patterns, your reactions to everyone else around you, and to yourself.

Because the alternative is automatic pilot. The subconscious mind running the show.

If that has led you to making the choices you want to make, great. Then you would be already doing all you want to be doing!

If it hasn't, then this is the work to give yourself a choice where the subconscious mind has taken that away from you.

Showing up for yourself isn't about rushing.

It isn't about being perfect, or about doing it all straight away.

It can feel overwhelming in the beginning. Your mind is working so hard to keep you safe and remember. But remind yourself you're ok. Do a lovely getting present exercise to remind you of where you are right now (including my noticing one below).

Take it slowly. One day, one step, one pattern. You're never 'behind' in life.

You are exactly where you need to be to see what you need to see.

The Daily Insight

Healing is a returning home to yourself.

What triggers you?

I want you to get curious about your triggers and experiment with them. Triggers are your teachers if you can allow them to be.

They are your subconscious mind jumping to attention to protect you. It will be deeply rooted in your reactionary past, and without noticing... and question them when they come up, they will continue to dictate your behaviour in the present. And they will be automatic... those autonomic nervous system responses.

Taking responsibility for what occurs inside of you is a part of healing.

Usually in our emotionally unintelligent and reactive state, we jump to blame others for causing it and we totally defend it within ourselves. But if you can get curious about them being yours... a remnant of your past, you will start to see them differently.

Can you start to notice your triggers? They are what I like to call your first responders. The feeling is intense, and your mind feels crazy. So obvious when we become aware of it... but hard to see until we are.

Can you practise sitting in that and not reacting, until you have all the pieces to the story? Can you slow yourself down - mind and body - so you can get to decide your reaction instead of it? It is hard at first. That's ok. It's meant to be. Can you welcome it?

Acknowledge it for being there to protect you from your past?

And allowing yourself to be teachable... to become conscious as to when you're reactive, is going to be what takes you there.

The world outside of you is what it is.

You can't change it to change a feeling within you.

And if you spend your life trying, you will get nowhere but exhausted and never find peace of mind.

Great stuff to reflect on in your journal. It takes a lot of awareness and practice to be able to sit and not react when these super uncomfortable feelings come up.

But this is the work you're doing. The more conscious you become, the more choices you will have.

"We may not be responsible for the world that created our minds, but we can take

responsibility for the mind with which we create our world." Gabor Mate.

The Daily Insight

It's cold here in Melbourne. I personally love the changeable weather that we have here. When I was learning how we all work, the weather was a beautiful teacher.

Maybe it could also be yours.

Just like the weather, our moods, feelings, thoughts, and emotions are constantly in flux as well. Whether we notice it or not, they're changing constantly. That is what is known as our 'psychology'. All the stuff that has come through our minds since we've arrived here.

What I would love you to start to notice is what is underneath all of that. Underneath all the clouds, wind, rain and turmoil. Underneath your psychology.

Which is the sun of your being.

Your inner well-being, your inner knowing, that is always there, never changing and can never be destroyed.

We would never question that the sun has gone, even on the darkest of days. It's always there shining brightly behind all that weather.

So is yours, beneath all your psychology.

Seeing who I was from that perspective, rather than what was currently going on in my mind, changed everything. Even the stuff that came up often and had created what I had thought was a permanent part of my personality.

I often had negative thoughts, but I wasn't negative.

I often had anxious thoughts, but I wasn't an anxious person. I often had stressful thoughts, but I wasn't a stressful person.

I often had habitual, and repetitive thoughts to do a certain behaviour, but that wasn't who I was either.

Those lightbulb moments (there were many when I really started looking!) changed everything for me.

Because if I wasn't all those things that I 'thought', well then, truly who was I? I still feel a thrill and joy in my heart at that possibility!

I guess I was whoever I wanted to be, whoever I wanted to create at any moment. Who I had been all my life didn't have to define me at all!

All I had to do was to see my beautiful, complete, and healed self already shining in there, regardless of the weather I was experiencing. And whatever the weather, I

didn't have to take it too seriously, as I knew it would change, and I knew it wasn't who I was.

I could start to show up to any moment more present to who I truly was and respond to the people and events around me... not to my weather.

What a relief that was for me to see. I wasn't broken, I wasn't lacking, I wasn't incomplete, I wasn't whatever label had been created for me or I had created for myself. I was me.

That's when it became important for me to work out my values. What my heart wanted. Which was so much easier to do once I saw I wasn't anything my mind told me I was.

How I wanted to treat myself and others around me. My values became my inner compass. My inner light is always there to guide me. By the way, it had been always there my whole life... I had just disconnected from it through the course of my living and the louder my psychology became, the less I could hear my own sunshine.

I didn't have to change my psychology... just like we never have to change the weather. That's not on us. We may just grab an extra jumper or an umbrella, but we know it will change.

All I had to do was to remember who I truly was. You are the same.

The Daily Insight

Do you find yourself frequently expressing that you have 'no time' to do what you know is required?

In a life crowded with demands and the legitimate needs of other people, time for yourself can seem the most elusive gift possible.

But it may also be the most essential.

When I've worked with clients who claim they have no time, I've encouraged an honest inventory of their schedules. Usually time does appear, but it may mean making a sacrifice... not as much social media or TV, getting up 20 mins earlier (mornings before my family is up are now so precious to me, yet this only happened in the last year), not taking work home, using 'waiting time' productively, turning a bath into mindfulness, lowering your standards of housework and what needs 'to be done'.

People who take time to 'be' daily are measurably more productive, better listeners, less stressed, more alive and more resilient.

This is in part because someone who believes that they have 'no time' is living under the delusion that they are a slave to other people's

agenda. This is never true (it's just unquestioned), and it is depressing.

Taking back control of your time even in a small way is a crucial act of healing and reconnecting with yourself. And it leads to other choices.

Meditation, walking, gardening, reading, listening to music, or just sitting and taking in the present moment are heart choices that help to restore us to 'ourselves'. They direct us inward - home - and help to put us back in touch with who we really are.

Looking at it that way, the time you give to could be the most important investment you make each day.

The Daily Insight

Choosing healing, no matter what you're feeling, is at the heart of change.

In the beginning, we won't 'feel' like it. Our brain will be coming up with so many reasons as to why staying where we are is a way better idea. The excuses, not the right time, the whatever... all normal, and all stuff we must step over to move forward. And it's all of these thoughts (both conscious and subconscious), that create the feeling we sit in.

It's so freeing to see we can do what needs to be done whether or not we 'feel' like it. And it is in the doing that our feelings, motivations, and energy change.

Engaging more consciously and constructively with our outer world – being more present to the reality of what is – is a sign things are shifting. The ability to notice what your mind says, but instead choosing to keep your attention on your outer world, is what you're aiming for.

The more you do this, the more you will feel connected to an inner knowing that you're driving your life... rather than feeling like you're drifting or something else is plotting your course.

All minds are full of chatter 24/7.

But the more you engage outside of it, the more in the background it will become. And the less it will continue to drive your choices in your day.

The Daily Insight

You are not a problem to be solved.

Please hear me out because your mind may instantly disagree. But what if I'm right?

What if you already have all you need to reconnect back to your mental well-being? You know... that place inside of you that is there underneath all your psychology, and when you're in there, feels like peace.

Einstein once famously said, "you can't solve a problem at the same level of thinking that created the problem."

Yet... that's what our minds want to jump to do. See all the things we do 'wrong' in our lives and jump in to try and solve them with the intellect.

That looks like constant reading, learning, anxiously trying to find that magic pill that will give you relief from your habit. All the things that create a sped up and anxious feeling - because we feel lost - which leads to us making poorer choices simply because we don't have the consciousness to access the choices available. And for most then, we simply don't do the work. We do all we can to avoid it. Innocently of course. We don't want to feel any

more pain than we've been feeling for as long as we can remember.

The only problem with that is it gets you nowhere, and your mind just goes deeper into the illusion that must solve 'you'.

I want you to just stop if you can this week trying to solve your problems. Park what you think is your problem(s) 'over there'. Don't worry, you can always go back to them in a week and continue the same path to solve yourself if you need to.

But I want you to see if you can see something new when you're not actively 'trying' to solve your thought created problem.

I realise this may seem a little scary - of course anything we do outside of that part of the brain that wants to constantly drive you, will feel that way. It may say "but without my constant working on it, I will give up." Or even if you think that "there's no way you can do that because without your constant focus on your problem, you won't have any control."

These tricks are all designed to stop you increasing your conscious awareness, which then may lead to you doing that risky thing called change.

Did you ever squish your nose up onto the window as a kid to try and see more inside?

This is kind of like what humans do when they're trying to solve their own problem. Only thing is that when we do that, we're not creating any space for insight... and it's insight that Einstein knew would change the level of thinking. It takes up that elevator of awareness so you can see more... so you can access all the choices you really do have.

When we step back from what we're trying to solve, we allow space for us to tap into the universal internet we're all automatically connected with. That place where we find a better feeling, more peace, and lots of insights we can follow.

Sure, intellectual knowledge is important. But it's not where the answers are for what you're seeking.

They're already within you. You already know it all. You just can't hear it because of your sped up busy mind, hell bent on solving you for you.

I can't tell you how many times I've talked to people who know this. They even tell others to do this. They've got more knowledge than me on virtually every subject related to health.

And yet.

They still can't stop doing their habits. They still feel like they're not directing their own life. They feel like a failure and they're full of shame.

But they haven't done the inner work. The inner work of stepping back from that part of the mind that wants to solve it all. They haven't stepped back from the window to get a good view of the entire house.

There's a story that goes, if you lost your keys inside the house, and yet you only searched for them outside, you will never find them no matter how hard you look.

The same for us all. The answers you seek are already within you. You must stop searching outside of yourself to find that which can only be accessed within.

So can you park your 'trying' and 'learning' and 'searching' to solve yourself for a little bit?

You may just see some things that will shift you.

You may even find life becomes a little more (or a lot more) peaceful, you're not as tired from all that brain work, and you start to notice a whole lot more good stuff that's around you. All of which will lead to you seeing what's already available to you.

Wouldn't that be worth pushing through that discomfort just for a moment, taking your hands off the wheel?

Yes, we are built to fly. You just need to see you already have wings.

The Daily Insight

Have you ever thought about what a feeling is?

I really hadn't much until my own healing journey. But they run our lives, as nearly everything we do is for the purpose of feeling more of what we like, and less of what we don't.

Think about holidays and cleaning. Both are done because of a feeling you want to feel, or those you want to avoid feeling if you were not to do those things.

They run our lives and decisions and it seems we're all in an endless search for how to have more of the good stuff, and less of the bad.

But do you know what they are, what they're made of, and how they work?

The way I've been shown is that feelings are fluctuations of energy to which our mind attaches words and stories.

Our left brain interprets, labels, and defines the energy that comes through us. So, when we talk about feelings and emotions, we're experiencing two things: the movement of energy, plus our mind's commentary on that energy. A subjective based story about that energy.

Feelings are the felt part of thought.

When the energy moving through you is low and your mind is thinking about your pet that has passed, your mind calls the energy sadness. When your mind experiences low energy as stagnant and unchanging it might be called depression. When your mind embraces low energy, you might say you're feeling peaceful.

When the energy is faster and you're about to do some public speaking, your mind might call it nervousness. That same energy on a roller coaster might be exhilarating.

The same one energy is the source of everything.

How you experience it in any given moment is down to the interpretative story your mind happens to tell you. It interprets and labels in an instant, all for it to make sense of life for you and in its attempts to keep you safe (all the stuff we did last year... we will revisit this again soon).

Fluctuating energy isn't good or bad, comfortable, or uncomfortable... in and of itself. It is just energy.

The meaning our mind attaches to it is what leads us to like or dislike what we feel.

And it's what we choose to do with those feelings that then in turn dictates our behaviour.

But do we have to do anything about it?

Watch your mind want to dissect this. Let it do its thing, but if you can stay curious, this understanding could free you from being a slave to your feelings and allow you to step into the life of your dreams.

My book is all pointing you towards this understanding. Much more to come.

Be kind to yourself and enjoy some times for peaceful reflections.

the Daily Insight

My backseat driver, lizard brain (or whatever you wish to call it) has finally gone quiet.

I have been making all healing choices after being a bit more relaxed while on holidays. It's been effortless, and also, I've finally noticed that the urge to eat something sweet after a meal has totally gone quiet.

That was... until today.

Today it started again, out of the blue, for no reason. What was hilarious and had me gripped with curiosity, was it was a different thought story too. One I hadn't ever heard before. Oh boy I got excited and curious at this new one and where it was coming from! Want to know what it was?

"Come on, you're too skinny now from all that walking you're doing... have some Old Gold Chocolate."

Which we have in the house for my kids and hubby. Ohhhh Habitual part of my brain, YOU ARE GOOD!!!!!

But I see you before you even see me now. And because I have ZERO fear of you, you have no power over me at all.

Some habitual pathways in our brain - because they are so well worn - can take years to quieten down. We strengthen the pathway every time we act... and when we see the little minion for what it is and let it go, it weakens.

But does it ever go totally silent?

I expect not. I suspect it's there ready to spring into action at any moment due to who knows what, how or why.

I expect not. I suspect it's there ready to spring into action at any moment due to who knows what, how or why.

Our job is merely to put it in its rightful place. Watch it, tease it, and tell it that it won't have its way with you anymore.

You're all ready to see this stuff in a deep way. It is life changing and has transformed my life more than anything else I've ever done.

A shadow of a thought.

As feelings are what dominate our lives, it makes sense to really understand what they are and where they're coming from.

Last Friday I suggested to you they were simply energy that our mind has attached thoughts and stories to. Let's look a little deeper.

When we're talking about feelings and emotions, we're experiencing 2 things.

The movement of energy

Our mind's commentary on that energy.

Feelings are the 'felt' part of thought.

Your mind interprets and labels in an instant, all because it's doing its job like a champ, which is to make sense of life for you, and keep you safe.

It's neither good nor bad... it's simply energy.

And... They are constantly changing. The root of the word emotion is 'in motion'. But it doesn't always seem like our feelings change quickly does it. In part because the labels become deeply habitual and conditioned.

And because we innocently misunderstand how our experience works, it leads us to mistakenly take these habitual interpretations as truth. They are not 'truth', they're energy with a label.

Feelings are not states that can ever exist outside of thought. While the thought may be hidden from your awareness, and your mind is pointing only to the feelings, they cannot live without an attached thought.

Fear, insecurity, shame, cravings, excitement... don't come through your body. Energy does. And then your mind slaps a label on it and determines what you experience.

That's probably the most important sentence for the day, so read it a few times.

When you see that the label is not as real or meaningful as it appears, that it's only a mind doing what minds do, feelings don't 'feel' quite the same.

Can you imagine how your life might start to look different if you weren't afraid of any feeling?

Just putting that one out there.

The Daily Insight

Moving from the 'me' to the 'we'.

What helped me greatly during my healing was looking at understanding more of what was relevant to all, not just me.

What I had thought was so much just a problem that was relevant only to me - my problem, my habits, my worries, my stress, my unhappiness - I started to see was quite universal.

When I started to wake up to where my own experience of life was coming from, I started to see that everyone else's worked the same way.

This is the magic of peeling back the curtain to see how the illusion works, instead of just being totally hoodwinked by the magic.

So, what did I deeply see when I peeled it all back and moved my focus off 'me' on to what was much more universal?

I saw that behind the layer of always shifting story and opinion, we all work in the same way. It's only the content that differs.

Our minds spit out repetitive stories, love to replay the past and predict the future.

Our minds have strong opinions that to us feel solid and meaningful but are always changing and contradicting themselves.

Our minds love drama and exaggeration. They relate everything back to the person they live with - our mind's world revolves around us.

They love certainty and efficiency. They create our 'who we are' story (and who we are not) and work 24/7 to protect its own creation.

What happened to me when I started to really see a shift in understanding? Well - initially I had to see that my mind was going to protest about me learning about it. Because it knew once I did, I would have to stop taking it so seriously.

It became easier and easier to not take it personally. I was able to create the space I needed to see it for what it was. Many of its habitual complaints, stories, fears, criticisms moved to the background, and became like white noise.

What was the biggest shift was when I saw that the feeling, I was sitting in often was totally changing. I felt many more moments of peace and a connection to something a lot quieter and deeper than what I was used to when living from that noise in my head.

I moved away from the details of what my mind was saying, to more of an understanding that a

mind is talking. The details of my thinking became a lot less relevant, interesting, and even worthy of my attention.

And because my focus was less on the details of my mind, I suffered less. I felt more at peace. I made better choices. I started to show up and really be with others.

My whole world shifted.

And yet... nothing outside of me changed one. single. bit. I got to know who I was by learning who I wasn't.

I wasn't all those stories in my head. And I began creating my life.

The Daily Insight

Healing is hard. Some days you want to just throw it all in and give up. Those days are totally normal and all a part of the process. You learn to just ride through those days, doing the best you can. They don't last, and the more you allow yourself to just be in them, nothing to do but be kind to yourself, the quicker the energy will move through you.

Healing is a long, slow, 2 steps forward, 1 step back and a U-Turn process. It's never straight forward, and never happens as quickly as our mind thinks it should. That's why you need long-term support and space to experience it all as it comes.

We're healing the mind as well as the body.

While you started with me perhaps because you wanted to heal your body, you can't separate your body from your mind. They're intricately linked.

And healing needs to come from both directions.

Today I want to give you a bit of structure to help you see those urges for what they are. A product of a brain that is on a healing journey too. Here's a 3-step process you can learn, that

puts so much of what we've been talking about together.

ONE

Re-labelling. When we can catch the thought of wanting us to drive to the supermarket for a chocolate bar or urging us to make a choice that isn't healing, we need to relabel it as what it is. It's not true, it's not reality, even though it feels like a true NEED. You can try to say to yourself, "I'm only having an obsessive thought that I must do this need.

It's not real, and it's not true that I need this."

The feeling of urgency is that false thought being felt in my body.

The first step to any change is conscious intention and attention (not ignoring it and hoping it will just go away. It won't). Being fully aware - and not afraid - of all the sensations that look like you have no choice but to attend to that impulse. But with relabeling it as what it is, it will help to change those pathways. Remember it's not going to disappear - I've shown you that. But you can see it as no longer a need, even when your body is screaming at you that it is.

TWO

Put the blame squarely in the right place. Off you and onto the brain. It's your brain sending you false messages. Step one you are recognising the urges. Step two you state very clearly where it's coming from. Brain circuitry that was programmed a very long time ago when you were a child. It is a brain that is constantly hungry for dopamine or endorphins, which means it's sick. It's not your fault. It's not who you are. And you need to take the blame off you and put it squarely on the shoulders of a dysfunctional brain and nervous system telling your body you are not safe. This is why compassion is so fundamental to healing. If you keep blaming yourself, healing will be hard. But the urge is coming from there, it's just a momentary influx of energy. A ringing in your ears. See it, separate it from you. Name it. Tell it you've seen it now. Get on with your day.

THREE

Get on with your day is step 3. The feelings (energy) are not what hurt you. It's your reaction to them in your behaviour that does. So, step 3 is all about refocusing. Have a list handy you can look to that has activities you love to do. Break the circuitry by doing something else. Dancing, singing, gardening, cold shower, anything you enjoy doing.

Teach your brain that you don't have to follow the urges (calls) it sends out. This is the "free won't" we all have - I am free to choose

something else when I've done the work of steps 1 and 2.

If you're struggling with eating/ drinking/ overthinking/ anxious thoughts/ overwhelmed thoughts/ worry... these simple steps will help you. Write them down in a way that resonates with you. Make them simple. STOP when you notice the urge, or even when you notice you're right in it. Go through these mental steps even when the urge isn't there. Visualise it and prepare for when it comes.

Because it will come. But you can be prepared... and not afraid.

The Daily Insight

Insight changes behaviour... intellectual knowledge may not.

Knowledge gives you a fuller perspective on concepts... but it doesn't necessarily affect you personally. Insight, on the other hand, changes you from the inside out.

When you have a deep and personal insight about something, you see a new truth that tends to affect your behaviour... and it feels like you're not really having to 'try' that hard either.

Often, when we start trying to have magical insights, we don't find them. Usually that's because we're trying too hard to find them or we're looking for the big lightbulb moments to happen... but they are rare too (but can happen). You might not even realise at all until your behaviour changes or life simply starts to feel different in some relatively subtle or indescribable way.

It sort of looks like 'nothing changes, yet everything is different.'

Creating the space for insight is how insights happen. Giving our intellect a break at having to solve and run our life for us. Stopping the job of thinking so 'hard' about your 'problem', and

when new information comes to you, letting it just wash over you without judgement or evaluation.

Without us even knowing it sometimes, we tend to either just keep confirming or disconfirming what we already know. When we do this, it lets our intellect evaluate or judge what we see or hear, instead of just allowing it to come in.

You may notice that beautiful part of your brain whose job it is to jump in and analyse it for you... but see if you can resist and just watch it with curiosity.

That witnessing is a game changer.

It allows you to be much more open, curious, and inspired, and with a less active mind... guess what? You will be more likely to hear things that you wouldn't otherwise hear... and the information will land in a deeper way.

This is the start of seeing who you are beyond your habits, thoughts, and emotions. A connection with that place that 'feels like home.' No longer needing to be anywhere else in life other than where you are. No longer needing to prove your worth to yourself or anyone else.

That place where we become connected to an inner deeper knowing that will be your guide on this short and thrilling rollercoaster ride, we call life.

That inner compass that gifts you with that trust in yourself to handle whatever is thrown your way.

I know some of you have felt glimpses of this place. If you haven't, that's ok.

It's there waiting for you, when you're ready to let go of the illusion of control that an active mind gives us.

The Daily Insight

What if your habit isn't personal?

Hear me out on this one - get out your considering cup - because your mind makes everything personal remember? So, this may take a little bit of considering before you step past your own thinking to even consider this.

Seeing my own habit(s) as not who I am was a huge part of my healing, and it transformed my relationship to them.

And it's probably where I break ranks with 'traditional' views of addiction treatments that put you in the equation in a very meaningful way. Something is 'lacking' or wrong with you in some way, and that's why you have your habit. Your habit is who you are, and you have to own it. Well, in my experience, that just keeps you living in fear of it. Let me explain further.

What if it's not like that at all, and your habit has nothing to do with you? What if your urges (which we're learning not to fear) are providing you with helpful information? What if your habit has nothing to do with your character or circumstances?

Our habits are rarely about pleasure. They're far more likely to be about avoidance. Something

we do to avoid discomfort. The urge feels uncomfortable, and we act on our habit to feel a release from that urge.

They are thought energy (not always ones that we notice) that feel compelling... but are quite impersonal.

We live in a steady stream of thought 24/7. Hopefully you're becoming a whole lot more aware of that. These thoughts aren't 'you' - they are simply life flowing through you. And we know it's all flowing, coming and going.

In my innocence, I unknowingly set my habit in motion with my thinking ABOUT my thinking, and with what I believed about my urges. Which I thought were dangerous, personal, unbearable, permanent... which meant I would naturally follow them. I didn't see choice in those moments... until I started to understand thought... and how it really didn't have anything to do with me.

No habit could ever be an indicator of your worth as a human being. Please read that a few times. Your worth is NOT tied to your habit.

Seeing that, and them only being passing thought, it became so much easier for me to dismiss them and let them pass.

The feeling (energy) you experience when you have an urge to do your habit is a helpful

warning sign. That dashboard on your car engine telling you something needs your attention.

It's telling you to slow down and become suspicious of the way you are using your power of thought. Because we are only ever living in a feeling of our own thoughts - and urges are just one type of thinking - the tension you feel is simply a reflection of a busy mind.

And boy oh boy I totally get how busy it can be in there... and how life totally changes when we see we don't have to pay attention to any of it! What a relief it was for me (and many who have gone through the habit change series).

—> Your mind clears of thought naturally on its own, and the presence of your urge is an invitation to step back, wait, and let your mind slow down. <—

Focus on your mind/body healing practices instead of that busy mind! Focus on your life that's right in front of you now...

Apparently, humans are the only creatures who speed up when we're lost. Other creatures stop and wait to regain their bearings. We rush forward, push through, speed up... thinking that doing more is where the answers lie.

But the answers always live in doing less. In slowing down, so we can hear our own guidance

system speak... that beautiful thing we all have called wisdom.

When I deeply saw that my habit was nothing more than an innocent misunderstanding, I started to change my relationship to it. It was never about the thoughts that were coming up... it was always about my reaction to them. My deep fear that they were personal, all about me, and all about who I was as a human being. And that if I didn't obey them, my life would be under threat.

One thing I know for certain... it's never been about me at all. My character, my lack of willpower, my lack of 'something.'

The same is true for you.

What it was (and still is) is a valuable warning sign that I'm super grateful I know about now.

Insights lead to a deep, lasting change. And it builds trust in you.

Fact based learning new knowledge is an active and contextual process, that we gather through active learning. We read, listen, rehearse, memorise. It's hugely important to us to know things, and in the context of lifestyle change, very important. We do need to learn the correct knowledge about our physiology and unlearn all the BS we've been taught.

But when it comes to behaviour change, we have to go deeper than that. That's what insight gives us. A deeper understanding of the way you see things in your life.

And it feels very different from knowing something 'intellectually.'

My deeper insights into who I was beyond my habits and thoughts were game changers. Seeing I could be anything I wanted to be, and the only thing in my way was my attachment to a thought. That thought I had carried which was handed down to me that I wasn't smart enough to be a vet, totally started to vaporise in front of my eyes when I saw the truth of thought. That unquestioned thought/feeling that said I wasn't ok unless I drank every night, the thought that

said I needed food to relieve me, that feeling that felt like I had to do what others were doing because I didn't want to be seen. All of them started to look like the brain junk they are.

With insight, I saw that none of them were true, and they never even had been true. They were simply stories my mind had created to keep me safe.

I was starting to wake up to where my experience of life was coming from... and at first that was super scary. I felt like I was stepping out over a cliff without any safety net. That's what my mind was saying to me anyway!

But there is always a safety net... you've always got your own back... you just don't know it.

How much does your subconscious mind hate insights? With passion. It will do all it can to stop you stepping out from your intellect to have them. Hence why it feels so hard in the beginning.

But it is the only way to free yourself from the conditioning and limiting beliefs of your mind, and step into the life you want... for YOU. Regret free living, remember?

How do we create the space for insight? Well, unlike the active pursuit of intellectual knowledge, insights usually come about very passively. Something most of us are bad at

doing. Doing nothing feels like we're wasting our day. Again, more conditioned thinking.

How can we be wasting our time when we're creating space for the deep and lasting change we're wanting?

We know we need insight around our habit when we still feel like it has a hold over us. That you fear the experience of it, that it's something you must avoid at all costs, that you still don't 'trust' yourself. Trusting yourself, by the way, is ultimately what you're seeking.

When we haven't had insight, it will feel like we must follow the urge most of the time. Sometimes we may be able to white knuckle our way through it... but we're looking to go way deeper than white knuckling. That's all about the intellect.

Insight changes you from the inside out.

Intellectual knowledge isn't personal. When you have a deep, personal insight about something, the new truth tends to affect your behaviour.

Like seeing who I was beyond my habitual stories. Seeing I wasn't broken or didn't need fixing. Seeing that I had all I needed inside of me... I just had to let myself look, and I saw this truth. I still well up with emotions talking about how incredible it was to see I was living my life based on the illusions in my mind.

Seeing my habits in a totally different way was what helped me to stop letting them control my life. My urges started to look very impersonal and very separate from me and who I was. I started to see them as the brain junk they were, and by far the biggest insight I had was that I deeply saw I didn't have to fear them. I didn't have to fear any of my experiences in life. You can't force insight. But you can create the conditions.

Give your intellect a break. Let your mind off the hook for a bit! Being busy all the time won't allow you to see deeper. Avoiding your experience won't either.

Allow what comes to come and don't fear the experience. Notice, witness, watch. Name them, laugh at them, make fun of them! You won't die if you don't act. I promise. But you may shorten your life and affect the quality of it if you keep following it.

Stop avoiding feelings, urges, experiences. They ARE YOUR TEACHERS. You've nothing to fear from thoughts/feelings in and of themselves. It's how you react to them that matters. Are they worthy of your reaction? I severely doubt it.

Let your mind say what it wants, but step into your heart. Now is the time. "You are the curator of your own contentment."

Yes, you are. No one can do that for you. And contentment is found when you connect back to who you truly are... beyond the made-up stories of your mind.

Your brain and your habit.

How often does it feel like you have two minds when it comes to your habit. In a sense you do, because 2 parts of your brain are having a discussion. One wants you to do your habit, one is giving you all the reasons why you shouldn't.

To understand your habit a little in the context of the brain, let's look at it simply in terms of our lower brain and our higher brain. Neurologically, your habit lives in your lower brain. The lower brain is the oldest, most primitive part of the brain. Often, it's called the lizard brain or reptilian brain. This part of our brain is habitual and unintelligent. It has no capacity for logic or any kind of higher reasoning. This lizard part takes note of and acts out patterns.

It is also where the fight, flight or freeze response lives.

It is responsible for maintaining basic biological functions and ensuring our survival: it generates the drive for food, water, oxygen, as well as anything else it believes to be essential for our survival.

And this is what happens when there is a deeply ingrained habit. Your lower brain acts as if it IS

necessary for your survival. And because it believes our life is dependent upon it, it sends out strong urges for the behaviour, thought or substance involved in the habit. Which can be insanely hard to step back from when your habit is food - food IS needed for our survival, and that part of the brain will take sugar in bucketloads.

Side note: we are deeply wired for that quick energy glucose to prevent us from dying in our tribal days. We may have come across it via a beehive or the occasional sweet berry once or twice a year. And those who binged on it, survived. Now, it's everywhere but our brain hasn't changed. Which is why we must understand how to stop being hijacked by that primitive part of the brain.

It really can feel like you will die if you don't act. I can see and remember those feelings so strongly. There's no logic in there. Only pattern acting. It has essentially hijacked you.

This is where discipline and distraction don't stand a chance. Obeying seems like the only way to release the pressure.

The higher brain, on the other hand, is more sophisticated and more advanced than the lower brain. It is intelligent, logical, rational. It is the part of the brain that makes conscious and voluntary behaviour take place. It is through this part of your brain that insights come to you.

Where your wisdom/heart can be heard, and the part of the brain that tries to convince you not to act on your urge when your lower brain is wanting its fix.

When I started to understand the limitations of my lower brain, and the power of my wisdom, things started shifting. The lower brain, while it's producing urges and behaves as if it's saving your life, cannot act. Your higher brain is where the acting comes in.

Your thoughts can't make you open a bottle of wine or a packet of biscuits or walk to the fridge. Your voluntary behaviour, operating via your higher brain, is required for those things. The lizard broadcasts the message, and because I didn't know better, I convinced myself that I had no choice but to act.

I didn't know that I could choose what to do with those thoughts and feelings being broadcast. And the more I understood how all this works, that the power of choice does live within me, I started to see glimpses of this fact.

It is a choice. It may not feel like it is, but ultimately, it is.

Understanding the origin and nature of hijacked feelings starts to strip them of their power.

I did have control all along, but I just didn't know it. I had no idea dismissing thoughts was even an option.

My first step into understanding all of this came from a book, Brain Over Binge by Kathryn Hansen. It just progressed from there and I learnt way beyond just the understanding of the brain in its physical form. We will get to more of that soon.

But this was the information that gave me hope. Hope for the first time in a very long time that I can end my habit. That it wasn't going to be with me forever. That in fact... it wasn't even 'me'.

Hope is everything. I know hope has never gone when we can't see it. It's always there. Hope... and a plan.

Finally, both were coming into my field of vision.

the Daily Insight

The internal traffic lights.

Sharing today something that came from a client session yesterday. This client wanted to be able to have more awareness around being 'reactive', so she had more space to consider her reactions.

So, we came up with this. A state of mind traffic light system. She saw this as a great way to notice her feelings when they were starting to become habitual and reactive.

When the green light is there, you're feeling at peace. In the flow (or the 'zone'), the air is clear. Your responses and reactions from this place, you can trust.

When you start to notice your feelings become a little sharper and more intense – sometimes like they're rising up within you ready to explode, the orange light is your warning. Slow down, step back, only proceed when you can feel your nervous system slowing. Be cautious about your responses and reactions from this place. Your nervous system is narrowing your field of vision in response to the stress, and your choices are diminishing.

The red is when you're about to explode or react. This feels intense, you're angry, super stressed, panicking, sped up. STOP. Don't react. Step back, physically remove yourself and your mind from the situation. You are purely reactive in this state and your choices are none other than the ways it's always been done before. That lizard brain is leading the charge. Your job in this state, once you notice, is to just stop and not to react until your nervous system has relaxed. Switch to soothe. Remind yourself that whatever you're feeling will pass, and until then, choose NOT to do anything until you've regained your bearings. (Unless of course your life really is in danger).

Once you can feel your body relaxing, your mind will naturally become more expansive for you to consider your options. Is this choice in alignment with your values? Is it taking you towards or away from the life you are creating? Is it healing your mind and body or creating more damage?

"Each difficult moment has the potential to open my eyes and open my heart." Myla Kabat-Zinn.

The Daily Insight

Is your habit personal?

I know it often feels very much like it is, and we often hold onto it like it is very much a part of our identity. Even labelling ourselves as something related to our habit.

But I wonder.

Seeing mine as impersonal - not even about me, was another way it all started to shift and fall away. I had thought it was all because I was weak, lacking, broken or incomplete... but when curiosity got the better of me and I started to question if it was even about me at all... this is what I saw.

We all live with a steady stream of thought all day, 24/7. These thoughts aren't you; they are life flowing through you. Like the breaking news across the TV screen.

Given this universal truth, isn't it interesting then when we see that some thoughts are more worthy of our attention than others.

All thoughts occurring within you, like the breaking news headlines, come and go and are in motion by nature. You innocently, and unknowingly, set your habit in motion with your thinking about your thinking, and with what you

believe about your urges. When they look dangerous, personal, unbearable, or somehow permanent, you naturally tend to give in to them. You don't see choice, and the only way to make them go away is to act.

And in this innocence, we tend to create elaborate routines to try and avoid them even coming up (exhausting and unlikely to happen). We get busy doing everything we can to fix and free ourselves... yet perhaps it's all about understanding. Understanding that totally changes the way we view their presence.

Understanding that frees us from the grips of our fear of them...

This is what happened to me when I started to see them as passing thoughts. Not something I had to get in the ring with and fight. Not something I had to work out how to avoid at all costs. And not an indicator of my worth as a human being.

Underneath all of it was me. Underneath all of yours, is you.

The energy - feeling - you experience when your thoughts are passing through is a wonderful wise warning sign, we can pay attention to. The traffic light system.

The orange is telling you to slow down and become suspicious of the way you're using your

power of thought. The tension you feel is simply a reflection of a busy mind.

The presence of your habit is your invitation to step back, wait, and let your mind slow. What a gift this is when we start to notice it.

And how life can infinitely shift when we start to see our innate well-being, and who we really are, beyond all that habitual thought.

The Daily Insight

Why do you do what you do?

Chances are it often comes from an attempt to fill the not good enough story of your mind. You can't yet relax, but you will someday....

I would love you to challenge that you will ever get to this mystical 'someday' and be able to sit in that place where your mind will finally tell you that you are, indeed, good enough.

Minds just aren't designed to do that.

It's not designed to tell you that now is the perfect time to enjoy life. It will never tell you it's safe to slow down, stop or rest. Minds are in the business of 'doing'... not being.

Life lived on that hamster wheel of 'someday' will never end with a good enough feeling because of some outside thing you've accomplished. It can't. Your mind just won't let it.

This is why you will never reach it someday, simply because there is no such thing. It's a made-up thought based concept, and the minute you've achieved or accomplished something, your mind will begin the search for the next destination....

It constantly takes you away from who you are, always whole and at peace, to that conversation about what's missing. That you need to do more, you're not enough... and when we listen to it, we feel like we're lacking.

Your mind has been doing this from the minute it took over to navigate something scary in your life as a child. You. without even realising it, began and continue to look to your mind for ideas on how to stay safe and fill the void... but your mind is creating this illusion of a void in the first place.

It's always promising that 'this' will fill you with the feelings you want. It's always coming up with new ideas to keep its own creation alive.

And these new solutions feel good (only because your mind has shifted), because we feel that that 'destination' of some day is now possible thanks to a new thought created task we have set for ourselves. And our mind constantly looks to give you evidence to support its hypothesis.

Apparently, neuroscience research shows that of the 7 core instincts in the human brain (anger, fear, panic and grief, maternal care, pleasure, and lust, play and seeking), seeking is the one most significant. Mammals are rewarded with a dopamine hit for exploring their environment and seeking, and our brain evolved to look ahead and predict.

But just because this is the way it works, doesn't mean we have to follow it, especially when we see it just as 'what minds do' and we will never reach that someday place.

So, what to do?

Like so much of the work we are doing, we need to remember who we really are, beyond all the stories and thoughts of our needy mind.

You're already good enough. Always have been. You're exactly where you are meant to be. Do you even really care about those things that your mind is pointing you to do?

These are the things you need to ask your heart.

Who are you beyond the goals, desires, wishes, and fantasies? What if you took your focus off what your mind is saying and saw that no amount of outside achievement, or anything outside of you is going to fill that void... because there is no void.

Even though your mind will probably never stop spinning those stories - it's its job remember - like so much of what it says we can stop paying attention to it and start paying attention to our values. To now. To today. To start considering making choices from a place of already having reached this mystical 'someday' ... instead of from a place of lack.

"We don't create abundance; abundance is always present. We create limitations." Michael Neill.

There is no lack. There never has been.

the Daily Insight

When we start to become more aware of the feelings inside before we react to anything in life, we start to gain awareness of the fact that we always have access to choose.

This is why even becoming more aware is a choice. You must choose to notice what's going on inside you. Even this may be difficult when your subconscious mind wants to keep running your show.

You are now aware that this part of the brain can only produce commands. They may seem louder and stronger than you are, but they're not. They're not you, you're only experiencing them. There are urges... then there is you.

When you start to see that the only way an urge can be acted upon is if you choose to act on it, you will see another shift.

It's not that they go away immediately (there's no timeline for when urges fade) or that they start to feel painless. They will still feel uncomfortable in the beginning, especially when you are experiencing them.

But you will start to experience them differently because you now see them differently. Perhaps you notice the minions sending out their

commands, or you see that lizard, or however it may look to you.

We cannot decide on the presence of any thought within us. Trying to change our thinking is like being condemned to push a boulder up a hill, but never get there. We can't decide what comes in. In fact, the presence of urges, or any thought, isn't really our business.

What is our business, is that we have the choice to respect or act on those thoughts. This is where our freedom lives.

There is a point where you get to choose your behaviour before you act. Creating awareness of this is what gifts you with that choice. Integrate this with the traffic lights. The traffic lights help you become more aware, to notice... the choice point then asks you to consider whether what you choose is going to take you towards or away from you. Your values, your goal, the life you want to create.

So, noticing is everything.

We notice... then we consciously stop and consider our options and the alignment with our values. Revisiting what you value - how you want to treat yourself, others, and the world - is good to do regularly.

Here's an easy way to work out your values.

"What are the traits you want to pass on to your kids or any young people you have influence on?"

I ask you to consider the question "what sort of person do you want to be remembered as?" - hint: it will never be about your status, money, or external possessions.

The first few that come to mind are what matter to you. Don't over think it. You know it. These are what can guide you in any area of your life once you have a deep clarity and connection to them.

AND they are yours, and it all starts with YOU. No one can give you values. No one can tell you what to value.

Then no matter who or what shakes your snow globe, you have your anchor during the storm.

the Daily Insight

There is power in the pause.

Pausing before you act can change everything, and there are a couple of ways we can pause.

The purposeful pause we can do when we notice we've moved from green to orange - we're heading down or we're already in the weeds. A conscious pause that allows insight into your thoughts and feelings and where they're directing you, and conscious pause to consider whether that's aligned with your direction and values or not.

And this pause can happen at ANY time. Before you act, or during the act. It's simply when you notice you are acting in a way you don't want to.

Just setting that intention is what matters. You won't always do it - perfection is never the goal - but to keep trying is what matters.

This intentional pause is what we generally do in the beginning when we're learning the truth about our habit. But once we start to see who we are lies well beyond that, the pause may start to look different.

It's a little hard to explain how this happens, it's something you need to experience (like all of this). But over time, as my understanding totally

shifted from seeing my habitual thoughts as anything powerful or meaningful, my pause happened automatically.

Almost like it happened for me, rather than actively by me.

Seeing the urges as not 'me', not who I was, as simply thoughts I had repeatedly acted upon reoccurring, they just stopped feeling so compelling. That thought I had to have that wine became something that I noticed briefly but could totally see I didn't have to grab.

Imagine your thought as like a bus coming through. Why would you hop on the one not taking you towards your destination? Not only that, why would you hop on every bus that went past? How would you ever get anything else done, and how do you know where you will end up?

That's what it became like for me.

"Oh, here comes that bus again, but it's not my bus."

It does become effortless when you see thought in this way. You just see the ones clearly you want to let pass by.

There are simply no 'pause' rules, and I've seen over the years it tends to naturally move from more conscious to more automatic. It will

fluctuate constantly as you may slip in to different habits without noticing... and then you do start to notice. Any type of pause that allows you to tap back into your inbuilt resources, to consider, to see your next move and ensure it aligns, is excellent.

All that matters really is that you create the space between 'you' and your habit... enough space to allow you to make sure you're getting on your bus that's going to take you where you want to go.

So, is what you're about to say or do, or is that ruminating thought going around in your head, your bus? Where are you headed by staying on that one?

Trust me... there are billions of other buses available to you... you just need to get off the one you're on.

Love you.

The Daily Insight

"Many people mistakenly believe that circumstances make a person. They don't. Instead, they reveal him or her. Our circumstances don't define us; they represent our unique curriculum - our tests, challenges, and opportunities for personal growth, acceptance, and detachment.

Our success as a human being does not lie in our collection of possessions or accomplishments. It does not lie in the details of our predicament, but in how we deal with what we have and how we face our challenges, how we transform our unique curriculum into growth and into a life filled with love.

We have the capacity to manifest our own destiny, to create 'real magic' in our lives, to remove ego from our consciousness, and make love our top priority. To do these things, however, it's essential that we create an inner balance, a sense of harmony and equanimity within. Peace of mind is not the end of the road; it's the beginning.

Contentment enhances everything in our lives.

Life is not your enemy, but your thinking can be. Our minds are very powerful tools that can work for us or against us in any given moment. We

have a choice. We can learn to flow with life, with loving and patient acceptance, or we can struggle against it. We have the capacity to make the human experience all it can be.

We have, within us, the resources to live a happy, fulfilled life regardless of the challenges we face." Dr Wayne Dyer

Make space and time for slowing down and reflection as often as you can.

The Daily Insight

Much has been said about 'living in the moment.' It is one of the oldest and wisest pieces of advice for living a more peaceful life... and yet. Very few seem to be able to implement this critical principle in their daily lives.

I believe this seemingly simple concept is so elusive because the untrained mind is much like a puppy - it wanders off without realising where it's going! Before long, the puppy - just like our thoughts - gets away from us.

Dr Wayne Dyer demonstrates the importance of living in the moment with a powerful story. He suggests imagining yourself on a boat in the ocean and asking yourself three very important questions.

The first: what is the wake? The wake, of course, is the trail of water left behind as you move forward.

The second: what powers the boat? The answer here is that the present-moment energy of the engine is the power that makes the boat move - not yesterday's energy, not tomorrows, but the energy generated in the present moment.

Lastly, ask yourself: can the wake power the boat? The obvious answer here is an absolute

no. The wake is powerless. It was created by past energy and has no power in this moment. You see nothing more than the trail.

How this story applies to your life is obvious but extremely important in understanding the pursuit of peace of mind and your dreams.

Many people live as if the past is running their lives. The truth, however, is that just like the wake of the boat, your past is powerless. It's certainly true that what happened in your past and the challenges of your childhood did happen, and your mind created stories and beliefs in its attempt to protect you. And it's also true that your nervous system may be dysregulated and sending out signals of distress regularly... when there really isn't any threat or danger.

And all of this impacts the way you see life today.

But your past, as it exists today, is nothing more than the thoughts you have about it (conscious or otherwise). This doesn't diminish or ignore any of it but helps you to see the patterns as they arise, to be more the observer from the place of the present moment and helps to free you from the compulsion to hop on each thought bus or feeling that enters your body.

You can either look and then respond (hop on and let them take you where they want to go) or let them pass and wait for the next one.

The Daily Insight

We've become so used to the idea that much of what we don't like about ourselves, and our lives, can be quickly overcome with little effort on our part. But a change in our attitudes and behaviour is a very slow process that requires conscious and consistent effort.

We can't work at it all the time, but we notice when we don't - we drop back into auto pilot - we tend to see our old habits rise and take the lead. That's nothing to do with you, who you are, or any value judgement. That's about your humanness.

Examining your life and changing it for the better is a difficult process that requires you to take responsibility for your feelings - deciding what you need to do - then doing it.

Wishes and intentions are not actually change.

A common illusion by those seeking to change their lives is that it can be rapidly achieved. Once we 'know' what to do, it appears that we simply ought to be able to do it.

The most familiar of our behaviours are the ones generally most resistant to change - drinking, eating, smoking etc.

Here we need to understand the psychological power of a habit. Some are 'good' and life enhancing - many are not and become so entrenched within our lives and entangled with who we are and how we cope with life.

It's obvious to me that any process directed at changing, even just a little, our well-established patterns of thinking and behaving is going to be an extended one and will involve efforts at gaining insight, re-evaluating behaviours, and trying new approaches.

Under the best of circumstances, these changes take time.

To imagine that such traits can be changed overnight or as soon as we become aware of them is to discount the well-established strength of habits, and the slowness with which we translate new knowledge into behaviour.

When we think about things that alter our lives in a moment, nearly all are bad. Phone calls in the night, a diagnosis, loss of a job, loved ones passing. Apart from a last-minute goal or winning the lottery, it's hard to imagine sudden good news.

Virtually all the happiness and healing processes in our lives take time, usually a long time. Learning new things, changing old behaviours, building satisfying relationships etc.

This is why patience and determination are among life's primary virtues (which you can make your deeply held values).

In a society based on consumption, instant gratification is pervasive. Somewhere along the line in our history we became impatient people, expecting quick answers to all difficulties.

But the process of building has always been slow. The tension between simplicity and effort works itself out in our daily lives. It takes time for us to notice and see that in any moment we can choose which path to take.

And... if we believe in the sudden transformation illusion, we are less likely to pursue the harder and less immediately satisfying work of becoming the person we wish to be.

So, here's the role of time, patience, GRIT, and reflection in our lives. What we believe about how life works and our place in it will determine whether we can find a satisfying way to live through it.

There is much in here to contemplate and ask yourself what you believe.

The Daily Insight

Setting boundaries is something 99.9% of us need to explore.

Why is it important? Because as Dr Nicole LePera says, "they keep you physically balanced. They help you to connect with your intuitive self and are critical to experiencing authentic love. They provide the necessary foundation for every relationship you have - most importantly the one you have with yourself. They are the retaining walls that protect you from what feels inappropriate, unacceptable, inauthentic, or just plain not desired. When boundaries are in place, we feel safer to express our authentic wants and needs, we are better able to regulate our autonomic nervous system response, and we rid ourselves of the resentment that comes along with denying our essential needs (that happens when we betray ourselves over and over to be loved and accepted). Boundaries are essential. They are also scary as hell..."

When I was diagnosed with Hashimoto's, this was the work I did with my own coach that made all the difference. I had already done the diet, I had overcome my sugar and alcohol dependency, but... I was still living in the belief that I couldn't create boundaries because I hadn't questioned the deeply held belief that convinced me that my well-being lived outside

of me. This was where I started to understand that I was still living in a mental prison and not fully in control of my own life.

This is big stuff.

But it is the real stuff that if you can put your big adult shoes on and face that fear, it will ultimately free you.

Can you see how boundaries start within you, and spread? And clear boundaries of what you accept when it comes to how you treat yourself are an essential part of Thriving. To destroy and walk all over my body with poor choices would never happen now. Yet it was an almost daily event until I did this work.

The external contents of our world are always in flux. Life will continue to throw curve balls, unexpected events, unexpected happenings every single day.

It has always been like that, and always will continue like that. And the majority of that isn't in our control (even though we like to think it is and we spend a lot of energy trying to make it true).

What we get to decide is what we bring to the table. Our reaction and our attitude... the way we see what's being thrown our way.

That is always our responsibility and all that we truly can ever control.

The essence of healing is in seeing this and creating the opportunities to see more choice where we don't see we have choice, and then accepting and releasing that which we cannot change.

How do we do this?

By noticing. By slowing down. By becoming more aware of our thoughts and feelings. By releasing others to be responsible for their own thoughts and feelings.

By deeply seeing that we're only ever in control of what we bring to any situation in our life.

The rest is not up to us.

The Daily Insight

Who's the judge of what's ok and what's not, ok?

What's ok and what's not ok when it comes to setting boundaries?

If we find it hard to say no - or if we do we feel guilty for days, there may be something for you to hear in this.

Either way, it creates unpleasant feelings so we're kind of in a bind if that's what we're experiencing.

We know that there's only what you see to do moment to moment, and they are your only options to see. What you see is what you see.

Mostly we've been taught to go right towards doing something different. To focus on changing behaviour or feelings. But hopefully you're seeing that this is like trying to move an iceberg by just chipping away at the top. We need to look deeper at what's underneath the water.

Because when we see the whole thing differently, the tip (our behaviour) changes as well. Just seeing how the iceberg is a beautiful metaphor for how we work. All we and others can see is that tip. But there's a whole world underneath the water isn't there - just the same

as pulling back the curtain to see behind the magician's illusion.

Can we see the whole thing differently? Let's see if I can point you in that direction.

When we're asked to do something, what comes up is a whole lot of thinking.

"I don't want to seem unpleasant, rude or mean." "What should I do." "What if I say no and they get upset with me."

If someone asks you to do something and all you're focused on is what your mind is saying - then they are the only options you will see in that moment.

You will either suck it up and seem mean or you will say yes. Either way you're probably going to be living in a horrible feeling.

But... guess what. You're not stuck with that thought that comes up.

That habitual thought-created meaning of your experience is how your mind has created meaning of these experiences in the past for you, but it isn't true.

We feel it as if it's real, but it's not.

It's always only thought coming to life looking real, and full of shame or guilt or possible

rejection, or whatever your mind has created for you.

But it's a thought bus coming by. That's all.

We all have our thought habitual buses coming and going, but they're not ours, they're not our mind telling us anything that's true. It is simply repeating patterns, and in that moment, you get to hop on it... or not.

It is always how thought shows up for us.

Every time our mind goes to a label or a rule or a story, you don't have to hop on. It only feels like it is because it's been showing up, opening the door, and you've been hopping on it for so long that it feels like you, and it feels real.

But it's not.

When we start to see that it is optional, we gain access to more options. You're shifting the iceberg from the base because you're seeing the whole thing differently. Not just chiseling away at the top of what we 'should and shouldn't do' – which is all made up from our personal mind anyway. Not doing it to avoid certain feelings, or because we want to be loved etc etc.

We get to step back and see the whole picture then decide from a place of a whole lot more options, and choice... and a whole lot less 'should or shouldn't.'

You either say yes if you want to or you can. Or you say no.

And the thought buses can just keep riding on by. That includes the guilt bus.

"There is nothing more important to true growth than realise you are not the voice of the mind. You're the one who hears it." Michael Singer.

The Daily Insight

In a podcast interview recently, I was reminded how much I used to believe that food and alcohol were giving me stuff to help me navigate my life.

For many years I couldn't imagine that I could possibly get through raising my young children without alcohol helping me to relax at the end of a 'stressful' day. I also couldn't imagine ever seeing through the belief that I just had to eat certain foods because of the relief they brought. I reacted instantly to my internal emotions - to what life was throwing up.

I didn't question them; I just did whatever I saw to do to bring relief from what I was living in.

That relief lived in food and alcohol. For others it lives in complex daily routines and a myriad of other habits our mind has so helpfully created for us for us to be able to navigate life.

What started to gift me with the freedom from all my habits I didn't want any more was to see that these things didn't give me anything I had thought they did. They promised so much, but never delivered on that promise.

I had to step back from the specific habit I wanted to stop and see that all feeling was energy created in the moment, and none of it I

had to fear. I certainly didn't need to stop feeling it by acting. I just had to see it as the energy of a busy mind passing through me, and as soon as I did that, it was on its way out, and I got on with my day.

None of the things I did habitually - drinking, overeating, eating when I wasn't hungry - ever brought me pleasure. They're not things we innately want to do. I remember that first glass of alcohol and it was disgusting. And yes, perhaps a little bit of chocolate was pleasurable for a moment, but a whole block never was.

My mind had many stories attached to both food and alcohol that stopped me for so long from seeing what those habits were. My response to a habitual feeling that I didn't see couldn't be true, and if I didn't act, it would simply become too unbearable.

We have a massive capacity to see we are 'ok' in any experience. To see who we truly are, no matter what is coming through us.

When we know who we are and that we don't need anything externally to give or take us away from any feeling, we can start to see our habits from a different viewing point.

- we move up from the basement and our awareness expands.

Life was simply better without alcohol and eating a whole pile of junk food.

I did for a few years have a story I didn't see for a while about socially drinking and eating junk socially still being something I wanted to be able to do (probably in order to fit in and not have to experience the uncomfortable feelings that often arise from standing out).

But I eventually saw through those ones too.

I was ok no matter what story my mind was spinning, which was constantly searching for ways I could moderate my habit. Perhaps I could have a binge on ice cream and chips every now and again. Or perhaps I could still drink socially when I wanted.

Well perhaps I could have if I had wanted to, but none of those things do anything for me, so I just don't want to do it. No willpower required. I just needed to remember who I am when I notice what old stories my mind is spinning.

That's what I deeply saw.

Why would I want to entertain and engage in ways I could moderate something that just never gave me anything I thought it did?

It's all a made-up story. All of it.

Your job is simply a remembering of who you deeply are.

The Daily Insight

Such an interesting conversation this week with a client who intellectually and insightfully is starting to see her habits from a different perspective.

And yet... her body is still reacting as though there is a stress when it is used to seeing one, and she's getting frightened by that.

In my experience, you will intellectually and insightfully see your experiences in life differently, well before your body will let go of that automatic stress response. Your mind will get there well before your body will - remember that response is so automated, it will do it in response to factors you may never become aware of.

Which is ok, and just all how it works. It doesn't mean because you're experiencing the physiological stress response that you haven't got it yet, or that you're not healing, or that you're still broken, or whatever story your mind might attach to it.

It simply means your body hasn't yet caught up to the fact that where you once believed there was a threat, there now isn't. It will, it will just take time.

And you don't have to do anything with this, except notice it... remind your body that you're seeing it differently now, there's no threat, and step away.

Then make a choice to act from that place of conscious awareness instead of reacting to the 'threat.' Every time you do that, you're teaching your body that it's ok.

Unlearning the past, creating the future. One moment at a time.

Such a wonderful space to be in to start to notice what's automatic and reactive... and then make your conscious choices from that place.

The Daily Insight

The wisdom of worry.

We tend to worry a lot. About our kids, about our health, about whether it will work, about many things. Worrying is another job our mind likes to have.

I don't often remember lines from movies, but one line from the movie Bridge of Spies with Tom Hanks was memorable for me.

When a man is arrested and accused of being a Russian spy, his calm demeanor never changes. Tom as his lawyer trying to prevent him from being executed, asks him a couple of times during the movie, "Aren't you worried?" To which the man replies, "would it help?"

What a great question, and one we can ask ourselves when we notice our mind busy worrying a lot... does it help?

Worry is a natural result of evolution. That tribal brain again is relevant to understanding here. When our very distant relatives felt fear of an immediate threat, they took protective action, which was rewarded with surviving into the next moment. Apparently, scientists call this an 'immediate return' environment.

We know our brains haven't changed in the past 2000 years, but of course our environment has, and we now live in what's termed a 'delayed return' environment. There are very few immediate threats to our survival, and most of what we do (shopping, cooking, working) has a delayed return. They don't result in an immediate payoff, and it's not about immediate life or death.

Because of this, we have a bit of a mismatch going on. Our brain still behaves as though you might starve to death or be eaten by a lion at any moment - even though you have a cupboard full of food, and you only see lions in the zoo.

When your mind screams fear today, it's almost never in response to true danger. And because there is no immediate action for you to take (run or fight), the fear doesn't just rise and leave quickly, because there's simply nothing in front of you to immediately protect yourself from.

And here then comes worry.

What does your mind do? Jumps to interpreting fear in other ways, by imagining what might go wrong... which we all know, our minds just simply have no trouble filling in all the blanks.

Oh, how it loves a job to do. Minds hate uncertainty, so it will just spit out whatever it

can to provide possibilities, most of which aren't accurate.

The evolutionary and adaptive lifesaving feeling of fear that kept our ancestors alive in their immediate return environment looks like chronic anxiety and worry about things that aren't real in today's relatively safe world. Our minds spin stories full of details and emotion, and before long it looks like an inevitable reality. It creates a state of mind that makes it look so likely that those worries will come true.

Minds create our reality, and then say, "I didn't do it." It constantly pulls in evidence as proof of the stories it spins.

Here's the thing. If what happens in your world is something that your mind has said might, it won't have been because your mind knew it.

Life doesn't work in that way. Life only ever unfolds moment to moment... there's only now. And a mind, right now, creating stories and images and projecting them outwards into the world.

But they are not 'real things.'

They are thoughts.

I realised as a champion worrier from a very young age worrying that my parents would never come home when they went out, that

worrying had become such a part of my experience. And often I wasn't consciously aware of the thoughts.

But oh, my wise body was telling me what my mind was up to. I felt it. And when I started understanding this wisdom, I started to pay more attention (that traffic light system), and step back. This stepping back gave me some much needed 'psychological space' to assess the situation beyond the narrow limits of my fearful mind.

Worry is such a mask we wear. We mistake it for love, and it makes life look so much more confusing and complicated than it really is.

We think it's helpful because it 'prepares us' to solve real problems. But does it?

Everything a mind does is to help you survive. And our brain's negativity bias and constant predictions for our survival as a species... but worry is like a rocking chair. It gives your mind something to do, but it takes you nowhere except out of your gift of this present moment.

Worry doesn't prepare you to solve problems. How can it when the problems your mind is trying to solve aren't real? And it's not protective, in fact, it's the opposite. It fills your mind with scary scenarios that grab your attention so you're less able to access your innate creativity and common sense, which we

need to deal with what IS reality, which is the present moment. And it's making us very sick.

What is worry then?

It's the wisdom in our body telling us we're caught up in thought.

The reality of what eventually does happen in your life will happen as it does, and it will have nothing to do with your mind spinning stories.

What a beautiful system we have when we know it's there and we pay attention to it. Preparing can be helpful - worrying is not.

Peace of mind. It's always available to you. And you will feel it so much more often when you step into your wisdom, and away from the busyness of your mind.

The Daily Insight

When was the last time you laughed out loud? And I mean not just said LOL, actually laughed out loud.

While many of us treat humour as a minor distraction from the 'serious business of living' it is actually an important component of a thriving life.

Apparently if you ask most people if they have a sense of humour they will say yes (as well, people universally identify themselves as being good drivers even with a stack of evidence that they're not).

How easily can you remember a joke or come up with a funny story?

Many are so unaccustomed to finding anything funny that we've lost our capacity for surprise, that is the essence of humour.

What gives humour its power in our lives is that a capacity for laughter is one of the two characteristics that separates us from other animals (the other is to contemplate our own mortality).

The best humour is in some way directed at the human condition. To be able to experience fully the sadness and suffering that life so often

presents - and still find reasons to go on - is an act of courage encouraged by our ability to both love... and laugh.

To tolerate uncertainty (which is what is always forever present, and always will be, regardless of what your mind says), we must be able to cultivate daily moments of pleasure of which laughter is the ultimate.

There is so much evidence showing that humour heals. We know our health is influenced by what we think and feel about our daily lives.

Humour is also a beautiful way of connecting.

Pessimists and hypochondriacs, I guess are right in the long run. No one is getting out of here alive. But pessimism - like any attitude - is contained within a self-fulfilling prophecy. The attitude we reflect is often what we get back.

So, what makes you laugh? When was the last time you laughed? One of my teachers used to say if I haven't laughed by mid-morning, I'm taking it all too seriously.

My husband and I have some comedians we love to watch often and no matter what mood we're in or what's going on in our day, a good laugh lifts our spirits. Perhaps finding a few of those on YouTube to have on hand would be worthwhile for you too.

The seriousness of our lives and the world will still be there, but if we can find a way to laugh daily, the journey will be a bit more fun. Oh, and our health, relationships and our day might improve as well with all those feel-good chemicals. Which can only lead to more fulfilling actions.

Can you cultivate some laughter today?

The Daily Insight

What are the signs your self-awareness is growing?

You're starting to be able to feel your emotions as they come and go, being able to be in them without fear or reaction.

You're finding yourself becoming more accepting of your past, and noticing it shows up in your present through your mind and body reactions.

you're able to be more the observer of your thoughts, seeing them as 'not you' or 'who you are.'

You're noting the patterns of behaviour that show up repeatedly, and asking yourself what you need more of with kindness instead of berating yourself.

You're observing how it's your own thinking creating your internal emotions, not anything outside of you.

You're noticing and examining your inner narrative... and questioning the truth of it.

You're catching yourself more easily when you're on automatic pilot and reacting to your

subconscious mind, instead of being in the flow of your day.

You're becoming more content more often with being in this present moment. "There's nowhere you need to get to... you're already here."

Did you notice what your mind was saying when you read these? Did it compare? Did it tell you you're not where you should be? Did it throw up that you're not getting anywhere? What did it say? You could read the above again as the observer, and the student that you are... that we all are. If you can do that, you may see where you might need a little bit more focus.

The Daily Insight

You aren't your label, you just 'think' you are.

Let's look at being insecure for example. There is no such thing as insecurity, there are only insecure thoughts. What about anxiety? Same thing, we're not anxious, we just have anxious thinking.

When we start exploring who we are behind our psychology and all the labels, we often get so busy. Looking for how it should look and how it should feel. Your mind, as a part of its function, is doing its job to own this new experience, to do it for you, but it's not needed here, and you can remind it of that. Thanks, but you're not needed here.

Here's something to ponder.

What if everything you've been searching for naturally finds you when your mind falls quiet?

Minds love to generalise remember. Your brain's job is to know stuff, so it can predict stuff, so you can survive longer. It's in the survival game, not the 'peace of mind' game. Not the 'you're now good enough as you are' game. It's in many games that keep us convinced that we are something that we're not.

What could be more important for your mind to know than 'who you are'? That logical and linear machine in your head is totally invested in you having a stable and fixed personality.

Once your mind decides you're anxious for example, confirmation bias kicks in and you see proof of it everywhere.

But what about all the non-anxious experience that moves through you as well that you miss, dismiss, or consider it a fluke? And so, anxious experience repeats itself not because it's who you are... but because you think it's who you are.

Your mind seeks to validate its experience to bolster the identity it's creating for you. It seeks to validate its experience to create a sense of safety for you (totally an illusion).

You can replace anxiety with any label you have for yourself and see this in the same way.

But the "I am..." label is a summary of how this experience tends to show up for you. And it's an incomplete statement that is full of exceptions.

And until we see beyond all we have identified with throughout our lifetime, it will keep looking like the stuff arising in us is 'us' and 'who we are'.

It will continue to have boundaries and names that our mind recognises and labels with language. It will look solid and real and who we

are. And it will continue to keep us locked in the illusion of a safe life. Wow our minds are just so busy aren't they.

But what if the traits and labels you've identified with over the years are far more in flux and far less about 'you' than they seem?

That's where we enter a whole new ball game about what's possible when it comes to living our life. When it comes to breaking free from the mental prison we innocently live in, until we see we can step free from it.

And in understanding this, we get this opportunity if we're brave enough to take it. Because we must sit in a whole lot of unknowns when we look in this direction. I think that's super cool... but I didn't in the beginning.

Your understanding of 'you' and who you are is in that beautiful little baby on the day you were born.

Everything since then has been experience, and none of it is who. you. are.

Grab that considering cup if you need to but see if you can open up yourself to consider this as possible.

Because what are your alternatives?

The Daily Insight

A reminder about the importance of healing nutrition.

Because when we're disconnected from ourselves and focusing on and reacting to our emotions, most of us eat food that damages and makes it all worse.

We know clearly that the gut has a role in mood disorders and other mental health conditions such as depression, anxiety, Alzheimer's, and autism (read psychiatrist Dr Rachel Brown's book Metabolic Madness to learn more and look up nutritional psychiatrist Dr Georgia Ede: (www.diagnosisdiet.com.)

There are trillions of bacteria and other organisms in our gut, and these organisms influence our immune and metabolic health. Bacteria in your gut are responsible for producing neurotransmitters such as dopamine, noradrenaline, serotonin, and GABA. These basically tell our brain what to do.

Our gut and our nervous system interact directly via the gut brain axis, and the gut and the brain are physically connected via the vagus nerve.

What we eat has the power to either heal us or damage us.

All we talk about in terms of understanding our thoughts and gaining self-awareness of our patterns is designed to help you see you can make healing choices, regardless of what feeling you're sitting in. It's about reconnecting yourself with your body and listening to it... not the cravings of your mind. It's also about understanding that stress is an internally created event via your thinking, and that this directly impacts your whole body as well.

This is why we address healing the way we are. It goes well beyond diet, but you must use your understanding to make healing choices.

Getting off automatic pilot and being consciously present is so important when it comes to making food choices. So, before you eat, consciously get present and ask yourself whether your food choices are healing or damaging. Are you eating because of true hunger or because you're disconnected from your body and eating to fill a void, fix a feeling, or without any awareness at all.

Eating junk foods to manage stress is like throwing petrol instead of water on a fire you're trying to put out. It makes your entire body even more distressed.

It makes no sense at all.

Emotions

The flow of emotions.

Where does that even come from? Should we do something to stop it?

Why are we so uncomfortable to allow ourselves to 'feel'? What are we so afraid of?

Most of what we're afraid of comes from deep conditioning around what we're allowed to express, and what we're not.

'Suck it up' 'big boys/girls don't cry' 'crying is weak' 'showing your emotions is showing your weakness' 'showing love is weakness' blah blah blah.

There is no truth in any of that, no matter how deep our conditioning is around it.

What I've deeply seen, and have completely shared with you all, is that you don't have to fear any of it coming up.

It's a beautiful thing to feel it all in life. Not trying to hide it, push it away, or eat/drink it away, think it away.

All feeling and emotion comes from within us, it does not come from outside of us.

The energy moves through us, and as it comes through it bounces off in different directions. Sometimes we don't feel it that much, sometimes we feel it very deeply.

Like when we're climbing our own personal mountain.

What a gift it was for me to be able to feel that experience in such an intense way.

While we love to judge and label them as good, bad, should and shouldn't... they're all the same.

It's how life moves through us. It's not telling me something about me or my life, it's just life flooding through me. Like light through a window.

What do you do about it?

Why should you do anything about it? Anything that might occur to you is always ok. You feel it. You live it. You get through it.

But we just don't need to see any of it in a 'different' way or some socially acceptable 'certain' way.

We just need to see it for what it is.

This then automatically will change the way we see it. No judgement, no pushing it away, not focusing on any thinking you may have around it.

Just feeling it.

And marveling at this incredible gift we have as humans to 'feel' things.

"If the only thing people learned was not to be afraid of their experience, that alone would change the world." Sydney Banks.

The Daily Insight

Sometimes we feel so trapped in our experience.

Have you ever wished there was an off switch for your brain? I know I have, and I know you probably have since we started our work together and I've asked you to look in the direction I have.

We know it's all thought, but sometimes we feel trapped in it and just can't see the insight we need. The thoughts just loop around over and over, particularly thoughts that we label as worry and anxiety, not good enough, not fixed etc.

We all have been there - me too.

While there are things we can do that help... there is actually nothing we can do to make it stop. There's no magical insight, no technique, no strategy to make it all stop.

Can you read that again? There is no magical insight, no technique, no strategy to make it all stop.

And when we think there is, we just get led back up into our thinking to try and find more answers in a place where they don't exist.

Like that magical silver bullet that will give us the relief that we're craving and stop us from having to 'try so hard'. To finally feel 'fixed' so you don't have to 'work at it' anymore.

Swimming in all that thinking is just innocently keeping it all alive, and that's what we will keep experiencing when we do that.

What totally helped me is accepting that I can't change my internal experience and what my mind does.

Until we free ourselves from having to change or fix our experience, we will forever feel exhausted and constantly like we're 'lacking' or 'missing' something.

None of that is true for you. For any of us.

None of it is you remember. That thinking will talk about you in every way it can. The past, the future with YOU right in the middle of it.

And we get so caught up in that.

And that's when we just need to notice. Notice that we've got tangled up in it, we're believing it, we're scaring ourselves, taking it seriously.

And those feelings we feel are our wisdom telling us it's time to take a step back, remember? The warning lights. The beautiful inbuilt system we have that says, 'Hey Tracey,

you're all caught up in that thinking again... it's time to remind yourself of who you are.... And it's not found 'in there.'

It's so good at convincing us to buy it and get sucked in... it promises us it's helping us and there is some solution in there. But there never can be if we're feeling badly.

When we start to understand in a deeper way that it's not you, that you can't stop it, that it's just your computer brain doing its job, you do naturally start to sit in a more peaceful feeling. And it just carries on like white noise in the background.

And you naturally see what you need to see from a more peaceful place.

The answers are sitting there waiting, but you won't see them until you look away from the chatter of your mind.

But our ego just hates not constantly being in control and knowing it can do or control it all. That's why your brain will spit up the thoughts, "But how?? How?? Tell me how!"

There's no how.

There's only understanding.

Find peace with that, and the peace you are seeking will find you.

The Daily Insight

"Success is liking yourself,
liking what you do,
and liking how you do it."
Maya Angelou.

What do you deeply believe is required to be 'successful?'

Have you ever considered this to be it?

The Daily Insight

Values. Why bother finding yours? Why do they matter?

To me, values are what allows me to say with confidence I am living a life true to myself. They gift me with the ability to truly see in any moment that I get to decide how I show up.

They're not goals. We can still have goals (if we wish) but they're not values. They are the qualities you can bring to your life while you're working towards your goals.

To me, they are my compass. They keep me steadfast no matter who or what shakes my snow globe.

They fill that void when I know I don't want to be reactive in certain situations, and they are what I reflect on at the end of each day.

My goals are how present I am in my day, and whether I was able to act in accordance with my values.

Values are the qualities that you bring to how you treat yourself and others around you. They are your heart... not your head.

No one can give you values. They're yours. And there are no right ones or wrong ones.

But there are some values that, if we hold deeply in our heart, will gift us with the opportunity to totally change the way we experience our life – no matter what the circumstances.

The Daily Insight

The relapse.

"It's better not to give in. It takes ten times longer to put yourself back together again than it does to fall apart." The Hunger Games: Mockingjay.

You will know if this post is for you. If it's not for you now, it may be for you at some point, so maybe screenshot it and save it for when you might need it.

What gets in the way most is the fact we don't expect ourselves to experience a relapse.

We can't expect to heal years of using a substance like sugar and alcohol without ever using it again.

I don't like the word relapse or setback.

Because it comes with judgements, timelines, and stigma. None of which is particularly helpful when we're on the healing road. But all things our mind just loves to offer up.

But we cannot ignore the fact that the sugar or alcohol (or whatever it may be for you) monster may rise, more than a few times, on its journey to a final demise.

Just know, that even with the best of intentions and the strongest of commitments, you may, at some point, allow your drug back into your life.

And the more you can face this reality rather than running from it, the more you will use it for what it is... a teaching experience.

But these experiences are usually incredibly painful. I promise you; I know this.

The gremlins seem to awaken stronger than ever. You find yourself spiraling down to the weeds so quickly you appear lost to its power.

You may lose trust in your own judgement, resolve and strength. You may find yourself self-loathing, full of shame and in despair. So deep again it seems like healing isn't possible.

But recovering from substance abuse is a war, with the highest stakes imaginable. For me, the most terrifying thing when I relapsed was how easy it was to believe that, because of the relapse, I had lost the war. Society tells us if we're unable to stick to our decisions, we're weak. If we break promises, we can't be trusted. It's so easy to believe that making mistakes makes us useless. We figure if we "fall off that f***ing wagon" we may as well "go all the way" because it's "too late now." We feel beyond repair, no longer worth fixing. We pile up internal guilt, convinced we deserve the hatred of those we love. So, we punish ourselves with

more of our drug in a bid to numb ourselves from all the horror.

I have been there.

But it is a mistake to believe that by losing a battle, we have lost the war.

The truth is that each battle makes us stronger as long as we remain committed to a better tomorrow. We must fight this battle with compassion and forgiveness.

We must allow that lost battle to be a reminder of all the reasons we wanted to quit rather than an unforgivable mistake.

The relapse experience will remind you of why you stopped. Your body will hurt, your mind will be foggy, your guts will complain, and if it's drinking – you will remember how it felt to nurse a hangover. You will remember the internal struggles, the recrimination, the deception.

Let these experiences tell you a story of how far you've come. Let them be what they are, a steppingstone on your journey.

Sometimes we forget why we started on the path. The pain of using fades and we wonder if we can moderate it. Our mind offers up the idea that maybe we can. Maybe we're missing out. Maybe we're feeling isolated and disconnected. You wonder whether using again will bring you

back these connections and fill that void the substance used to fill for you.

But a substance can never heal these things.

And it's very hard to do this on your own, even though you may want to hide because of the shame. This is why we are here, and this group is designed as it is. Use it.

You can overcome this.

Let each temptation, each battle bring you closer to winning the war. Learn from each experience. Discover the truth about your drug and its role in your life.

Sugar. Carbs. Alcohol. It doesn't define you.

It does not give you your worth.

It is not who you are.

It will not fix your problems, solve your loneliness, or provide you with any answers that you seek.

This is a journey. Not a destination. It is a road that no one else can walk but you. These are choices that no one can make but you.

But know that by committing to a different future, no matter how many battles you have ahead of you, the war has already been won.

The Daily Insight

Now get them off the page and into your life. Values look great on the page.

It can also feel great to claim certain values as your own.

But none of that counts for anything if the values are not lived out. On the good days it's easy, but what about the not so good days?

They are your compass and can guide you in how you treat yourself first and foremost. They gain in 'value' to you when you allow them to support you.

When they shift the way you see a situation and how you respond to it.

We all value or at least say we do - goodness, kindness, honesty, truth, and freedom. We all value love.

But what grabs your attention and holds it? What drives your choices to which you give your attention, time, energy, and money to?

Whatever your answer, that is what you are valuing. Is there a disconnect between your heart and your actions?

A couple more questions for you to reflect on to really nail your personal values. What do you stand for?

What would other people assume you stand for, based on your actions, the decisions you make; what you talk about, what you spend your money on, and especially... the way you spend your time?

What would you like to stand for?

Addiction is NOT a moral failing. This belief keeps you locked in the cycle of shame. Addiction is an illness. Like cancer. Like type 2 diabetes. You need to heal. But you must get out of your own way to allow your body and mind to do that. It is NOT your fault. You're not weak. In fact, totally the opposite. You are powerful beyond measure. I offer a perspective of education and enlightenment, based on common sense and the most recent insights across psychology and neuroscience. A perspective I hope will empower and delight you, allowing you to forever change your relationship to anything that feels like it has a hold over you. What you are searching for is in this journey... not the destination. Embrace the journey.

"Sugar was once such a rare resource that nature decided we didn't need an off- switch - in other words, we can keep eating sugar without feeling full." David Gillespie, Sweet Poison.

Like with many addictions, we don't want to believe we have a problem until we well and truly do. Humans are an addictive species. Our motivation and learning of 'good' habits sit in the same place in the brain as addictions do.

I like to keep things simple and define addiction as "doing something on a regular basis we don't want to be doing."

I do not believe there are addictive people. I believe there are addictive substances, and anyone consuming them can become addicted.

Sugar being the most addictive substance - more addictive than cocaine - and of course our dealers are everywhere. Add on top of that the fact you're considered the abnormal one if you don't indulge, it is one of the hardest drugs to get off. And we must eat. And most of what we're told to eat is junk.

We mostly don't realise we have a problem with sugar until we try to cut back. Then we often close our mind to the reality of it. And sugar is carbs - processed carbs. The body doesn't metabolically see it as any different. So, it may be ice cream, or it may be crisps.

It is possible to stop being controlled by all of it. And I'm going to make a very strong case for why you probably want to rethink moderation. I really despise the term everything in moderation. It was designed to keep you hooked on their products. I fail to see how we can moderate poison, but that's just me.

I also believe we can learn a lot from the failings in how we have dealt with alcoholics. We need to keep our eyes open and honestly evaluate

what we can use with sugar addicts and what we can possibly do differently.

Alcohol is the same as sugar in my view. There is no safe limit. Like sugar, we've been convinced it must be a part of our lives and we have subconscious beliefs that we can't have fun or be in life without it. 'Those' people who end up as alcoholics - we often convince ourselves it could never be us. Yet alcohol is a huge problem, and if we're looking at sugar, we also need to look at drinking.

It takes courage to look at all this honestly.

But if we want to show up to life at our best, we must step into that quiet courage.

The Daily Insight

Rebuilding self-worth is found in the small daily things. How you show up for yourself, treat your physical body, handle your emotional terrain. Those small daily promises to ourselves, that we keep.

Self-worth starts when we take care of ourselves. Becoming worthy of it, in those small ways.

Many of us have developed patterns that are not self honouring.

To overcome these patterns, we need to become aware they exist.

We can't change what we can't see.

The Daily Insight

Lifestyle change doesn't happen just because you want it to. There are some fundamental things you need to address to change anything beyond the limitations of short-term willpower.

This looks like addressing deeply held, and often unconscious, beliefs about something we want to change.

Let's take giving up sugar for example. Sugar is addictive and a primary cause of poor health. We may learn that it's not good for us, and we decide we want to give it up, but unless we change our deep beliefs around what we think it's bringing us, we will be faced with an internal war. Our conscious mind might want us to give it up, but our subconscious mind won't. And it will keep sending out those signals and messages to keep it in your life... and your willpower has no chance against that in the longer term.

So, what's the answer?

There isn't only one answer, but there is an important piece that can help to end the internal war. Which is to firstly become aware of, and then to challenge, the beliefs of our subconscious mind.

If we believe we need sugar in our life, and in fact we're missing out on something important in life by having to 'give it up', it will keep controlling you.

But seeing it for what it is, an addictive poison that isn't giving you anything good allows you to challenge - and then change - the deeply held belief that in fact, it's giving you anything good in life.

From that perspective, we can start to see what we're gaining by removing it from our life, not what we're missing out on.

The same can be done with alcohol, processed foods, or anything you consume/do consistently, but you simply don't want to be doing anymore.

This is to me the most important puzzle piece that comes with taking the power back from addictive substances like sugar and alcohol. And it's one most people miss. But seeing your deep beliefs around consuming these substances - and challenging them based on the truth as to what these substances do to our body - helps to remove the temptation to have them.

And without the temptation, there is no addiction.

The Daily Insight

There's a quote on my website that says, "the day you stop running away from yourself is the day your life will change."

I've not really considered whether there is any scientific basis behind why so many of us tend to do this. But now with my study into understanding dopamine, I'm seeing what may be behind our desire to constantly distract ourselves from ourselves.

Dopamine is all about the pleasure pain balance. And we spend a lot of time and energy avoiding pain. We all seem to have all the right things, and yet, so many of us are not content. I have said this in my TEDx talk. "I had all the content, and yet... I wasn't content."

While so far, we've covered the many factors behind this, like our nervous system, nutrition, and gut health, connecting with our heart centred values, mindfulness etc., I want to take us down the dopamine rabbit hole to understand what's going on in our brain.

If we can take a bird's eye view of it, and step back from our own 'running away' activities for a moment, perhaps we will then add another layer of understanding to the truth that none of this is our fault.

With that layer removed, we can then get stuck into returning home to who we are, and we can finally stop running away from ourselves - stop running away to avoid any pain.

Allowing ourselves to be bored. Why are we so afraid of being bored? Because boredom forces us to come face to face with the bigger questions of meaning and purpose. And it's also an opportunity for discovery and invention.

Lockdowns highlighted this for me on a mass scale. We were forced to confront this, and we either did and we changed our lives and reevaluated our direction, or we didn't, spending the whole time distracting ourselves with all the things we do - phones, social media, earbuds, Netflix, eating, drinking, pills etc....

One word that's interesting in that quote on my website is 'decide.'

That's one thing you do have to do. You must choose to stop running. I have that quote on my website because I remember making that choice some 8 or so years ago.

It was only once I did that, I started to create the life I wanted.

I didn't know then what dopamine had done and was doing in my brain. And with what I'm now learning, I again get to see another layer of

healing that has gone on, without my even knowing it.

Some of you I know, have already decided. Perhaps some of you haven't yet.

The only question I would ask you to consider if you haven't, is If not now, then when?

Because your subconscious mind will always offer up reasons as to why you should wait. ALWAYS. It's never going to say... now. You - your conscious mind - must be the one to say enough. Now is the time.

You must decide if your subconscious mind is going to keep deciding the trajectory of your life, or you are now going to start taking over.

Some big choices.

But how cool to see we do have this choice.

The Daily Insight

Yesterday when recording my latest podcast, I was reminded of the actual moment I decided it was ok to just be 'me'.

What a weight was lifted off my shoulders in that single moment.

Even as I was learning all about conscious and the subconscious mind, the way we work, and the fact we innately have all we need inside us to thrive, I was still subconsciously trying to be like my 'teachers'.

Should I talk about it this way or that? Does it mean I shouldn't talk about that? How should I do or talk about anything?

That was so exhausting.

I can't remember the moment that gave me space for the insight, but I remember emailing one of my teachers and I said, I finally get it.

"I just need to be me."

Even writing this now - and saying it in my podcast recording yesterday - I well up.

It was literally the first time in my life I saw it was ok to simply be who I was. Speak my truth. Use my voice. Share how I saw to share. How it was

received by others was never even on me. My only job was to speak from my heart.

There is no right or wrong way. There is only the way.

Just like life. There is no right way or wrong way in life. There is only life. And you get to decide how you live it.

And there are only 2 choices.

Do you follow your automatic pilot and subconscious mind that is all about keeping you trapped in the past, but brings with it certainty, or. Do you follow your heart, which is all about your future and where you want to go? No certainty, just a connection with your truth.

As I wrote in Insight 66, "Life isn't about being like someone else. It's about being you. And who you are is that person when there isn't much in your mind."

You feel good with that person, and so do others. That's who you truly are. All the rest is just made-up stories of the mind.

The Daily Insight

A part of no longer running is the learning to be with our own thoughts. Without judgement.

Mindfulness practices are an important part of learning to no longer run, especially in the early days.

If your mind automatically jumps to "I hate mindfulness, I can't do it, I am not that type of person" ... that's not you, that's your subconscious mind keeping you from change. We must stop jumping to those foregone conclusions it has been making for you your whole life, and start to move towards a path, whether our mind wants to come along or not.

So many of us do our habit to distract ourselves from our own thoughts. And when we first stop doing that, our thoughts, emotions, and sensations come crashing down on us.

But we must confront this if we ever want to move past it. It's the only way.

We can learn to stop avoiding or distracting ourselves from these painful emotions by being willing to allow them to be there. To tolerate this normal part of being human, and to no longer fear it.

Have you met our **OWL**?

Observe (notice)

Willing (be willing to stop running and distracting)

L (lean in on your values instead)

Observing and being willing to allow it to be there. It can feel like these days last forever, but they won't if you stay committed to your heart.

Your mind begins to relax, and you begin to allow yourself to open up more. And with that, you see you can be ok with the present moment. You are ok in this present moment. You can live in it, tolerate it, and eventually even embrace it.

The Daily Insight

Calming your mind.

While putting together the videos and resources for the intensive one-month sugar fast this week, I was reminded of one of the mental barriers I gave myself when I was breaking up with sugar and alcohol.

I had become aware that for me, most of the time I ate or drank was from a very reactive state. I was totally in the weeds physically and mentally, and I didn't see any other way out other than to act.

So, one mental barrier I gave myself was I made the decision not to act from that place anymore. Instead, I would work on calming my mind (thus my nervous system).

Training yourself not to act from that place is a good strategy. Because we know from the weeds, the world looks murky. Our eyes have debris, and our choices are largely limited to those habitual ones we've developed in response to fear.

Reacting from that place is running. Running from the pain. And a big part of healing is making that choice not to run anymore.

Discovering for yourself what calms you most effectively and practising it faithfully, is a way to develop this skill. Of course, when you believe that the substance is what calms you - as I did

for many years - it requires you to challenge and readjust your beliefs based on the facts (your subconscious mind gives no crap about whether your beliefs are accurate or not).

In the moment to calm your mind, any of these options may help:

Paying attention to your breathing (slowing it will always bring a calm to your nervous system)

Checking your posture, and strengthening your body (I think I even pushed out a few push-ups and squats at times)

Reminding yourself you can do this, and remembering the new direction you're heading in

Refusing to be hurried

Writing some things down - remembering your values

Remembering an experience in the past where you've managed to calm your mind.

Focus on the calm, not the problem at hand. Once your nervous system is back in balance, your awareness of your access to choose will be far more increased.

The Daily Insight

What does this situation need?

A great little insight from watching Ted Lasso last night.

Stepping back and asking, "what does this situation need", helps give you access to the many resources we have innately to help us navigate life.

But to access them, we must see we can step back from our largely habitual and reactive responses to any situation we are in.

"My entire life has been one big reaction."

This is a line from my upcoming TEDx talk. I was the queen of reacting. Until I realised how limited being reactive was. It's from this place that we tend to make the same choices over and over because it's virtually impossible to access what else may be available.

And... when I lived my life from this place, I was so far away from myself. I was not living my own life... and that disconnect inside was a constant source of pain.

One simple change of thought can change everything. "What does this situation need?"

Ask yourself that and see what your wisdom offers up. Then follow that.

The Daily Insight

Values are so important as a compass for our life.

I've been so beautifully reminded of this in writing my talk for Melbourne's Road Show. We're never done with values.

They are there for us always, and when we notice that feeling that looks like we've lost our way a little, we can reconnect with our heart at any time to get some guidance.

When we know our mind is mostly putting out habitual, stale and fear driven stuff, following our heart feels a lot more like we're living the life we want to live.

We can choose to align our actions with our heart anytime we want to. A part of my talk says,

"we're all getting older, and time is passing, there is no choice in that. But we do get to choose the direction we take in our choices each day. We can choose based on our own short-term impulses... or we can choose based on our most deeply held values."

We're always choosing whether we are aware of it or not.

And heading in the direction of our heart centred values is what takes us to living that life that is true to ourselves.

When things go wrong (which they inevitably will). The idea that you are responsible for your own peace of mind can seem brutal. Life is not fair. We don't all get dealt the same hand. Even when we've done the healing work, we still feel far from great when life throws curve balls. Our kids get sick, partners lose jobs, life happens. I know my mood drops and I can feel overwhelmed and afraid when these things go on around me.

However, even in the toughest of times, I have choices about my response. I can collapse - or hold steady. I can meet the situation from a fearful place, or I can ask myself the vital question, "what does this situation need?" Or "what does this moment need?" Like I talked about last week. This 'wakes up' my inner strength, gives me space to remember my values, and allows me to bring my focus back onto the bigger picture.

Where the worry of the suffering of others drives my mood, I must make some tough decisions. If I allow their suffering to flood me, I am much less help to them than when I can be with them in their suffering without allowing it to totally overtake me.

This does not mean I am less loving or empathetic. The opposite. It can be the most loving response not to fall into the same place they are. I know how hard this can be. But here your steadiness is needed even more. The analogy would be taking off your life jacket so that you both drown, rather than keeping yours on to help the other person stay afloat.

There are no rules or timetable for moving through setbacks. Judgements of yourself and others never help the situation. All we can do is remember that we have an incredible number of resources that innately live within us to get through whatever life throws our way. We can choose our responses, no matter the feeling we're in. This is in fact how we reconnect with ourselves and keep on building that trust in ourselves.

Kind from the inside out. Kindness to others becomes meaningless when you are not also being kind to yourself.

While there are many chapters in our life where we don't have as much time to do what we want to do for ourselves, kindness is not just about doing. It is much more about a way of being. And it starts within.

Think deeply about what 'being kind to yourself' means to you. We may think about doing less, or living more simply, when we begin to think about being kinder to ourselves.

Sometimes though, for me, it may involve believing in yourself more, taking more risks, standing up more confidently for what you want and what you believe in, saying no more to make more room for yes. Maybe it may mean doing more, rather than less; or doing what you do with greater connection to your values. With more confidence, curiosity, and trust in you.

It may also mean getting back in touch with your senses; taking time to do things in a way that feels less hurried and more rewarding.

Most of all, it may mean engaging with life more deeply; allowing yourself to know what your

feelings are and to express them; behaving in ways that are authentic and open, rather than defensive and guarded.

Being kinder to yourself will always include monitoring how you talk to yourself. How you physically and mentally nurture yourself.

When your demands on yourself are great, or when you are picking at yourself or putting yourself down, you will feel... and express out the strain of that onto others around you.

To be kind to others, and to create a more peaceful and accepting atmosphere around yourself, you need to start exactly where you are.

The Daily Insight

What if shame can be healthy? I've recently had some insights on this after reading about the importance of (and very rare) 'radical honesty' in Dopamine Nation. I believe tapping into that feeling we know as 'shame' could help us become more honest with ourselves. To help us align more with our values, and to end the cognitive dissonance or that war within ourselves.

I believe it's a healthy thing to feel shame when we've done something wrong. It is healthy to know that you've done something wrong and face up to it. There are many people in our world who seem to have their shame switch permanently turned off - who are aggressive, defensive or self-pitying when they should feel shame. And everyone around them suffers for it. It is a trauma response and inside that behaviour is a small, frightened child. However, it doesn't excuse it and it is what happens when we don't heal from our trauma.

Shame is a powerful warning that harm has been caused - either to yourself, or others around you. Instead of ignoring it, pushing it away or excusing it, we can face it and honour it for the teacher that it is.

Self-respect doesn't diminish when we feel shame. Self-respect demands that you should clearly know right from wrong and make amends when needed.

It's so tempting to make excuses rather than amends (you made me do this for example, I've had such a hard day, I'm so stressed). But making excuses diminishes self-respect.

Self-respect requires that you:

Acknowledge what you've done.

Take responsibility for it.

Express your regret.

Genuinely resolve not to repeat this same mistake.

Make good when appropriate and move on. Note the move on part. It is an essential requirement if we're actually tapped into being a lifelong learner.

Making amends doesn't mean wallowing in self-pity (I'm so bad, I'm hopeless, I'm the worst parent in the world, how could you love someone like me etc.). Oh, how I floundered for so long in the pools of self-pity.

But self-pity does not build self-respect. It is, in fact, the enemy of self-respect.

It keeps you focused on yourself rather than recognising the consequence of your actions, and what you must do about it. It keeps you from recognising that you've veered off your values path, and then making that essential realignment.

It keeps you from being teachable and recognising the value of every experience for the teacher that it is.

What if someone has harmed or abused you, and you suspect you are carrying their shame? Please seek professional help. You did not cause the wrongdoing, and with help, you can come back to the essential goodness of who you are – and move on. And in fact, if you don't do that, then the generational cycle of shame that often exists, will likely continue.

The Daily Insight

Why do we make the choices that we make? Have you ever stopped and considered the answer to this question? Let me tell you.

Everything you do is driven by your own thinking. Most of it subconsciously, but nonetheless, it comes from within you.

You can only ever act from your own internal thoughts. And feelings reflect your thinking.

This is the only thing that is ever behind your actions.

And if we've spent a lot of our life - like I did until my 40s - making others responsible for our internal world, it can be quite confronting at first to accept this truth. But ultimately, this is where the freedom we're after lies, in deeply understanding this.

Yes, the outside world and others are influencers of course.

But no one or no 'thing' can put a thought or feeling into you. They are entirely yours to own.

Once we start to see the truth in this, we then get to dig a little deeper and look at what lies behind the choices we make. What drives those?

Well for many of us, it's a conditioned thought born of cultural conditioning, others' opinions of you, others' reactions to you, and how you have been able to survive as a child.

To remain loved.

And sadly, for many of us, this comes from a place of lack, not worthy, not good enough.

If what we do to live our lives comes from these dark places, we will never reach a place where we don't feel anything other than these things. Your mind will always agree with any deep belief you have that looks like this. Always. It's so deep and conditioned, and it will protect its creation at all costs.

But we can change this through the work you're doing here. With insight, understanding, and awareness.

And a conscious choice to follow your values - which must come from your HEART, not your head. You can't intellectualise your values, sorry. You can only feel them. If they don't make you feel... they're not your true values. And you will know if there is a disconnect. And so will others, as your actions won't reflect what you say your values are.

This is why 'values' work is so important.

So along with the witnessing and noticing you're starting to do, see if you can pull back the curtain and see what's living behind those choices and patterns for you.

Because here is the truth.

You are not lacking (you never have been). You are enough (always have been)

You are worthy (always have been) You are not broken (never have been).

Abundance lives in your heart. Your job is merely to sidestep all the layers of your mind and meet it.

"We don't create abundance. Abundance is always present. We create limitations." Michael Neill.

Happiness, or what I like to call it, peace of mind, is available to you right now. It lives underneath your deeply conditioned beliefs and thoughts. Your job is merely to look beyond your deep beliefs to see it.

The prevailing myth that we've all lived with that happiness comes when we reach our goals, have the right stuff, look the right way, is just that.

A myth.

We have been culturally programmed to think that peace of mind comes from outside of us, and it will come when we 'get somewhere' or 'have something.'

Those things outside can never create happiness. They may bump up your dopamine and serotonin levels for a bit, but it won't last.

It can't last.

Because it doesn't live outside of you.

It is an inside job. And when we can connect with it - beyond our deep beliefs that are colouring the way we're viewing the world, it will automatically affect the way we live our life.

In my own life, I found what we collectively call 'success' because I found myself first.

I spent most of my life trying to control the outside to fix the inside. Trying to gather all I could outside to feel happiness. But that was all

fueled by a deep belief that I wasn't worthy and had to do all this to become worthy.

Perhaps this is one of the biggest illusions we all innocently live under, and I for one am forever grateful I saw through this illusion. Imagine spending the rest of my life searching for what I was looking for in a place I was never going to find it?

Dr Wayne Dyer talks about this with the story of the keys. Imagine you lost your keys inside the house, but because the light was brighter outside, you just searched out there. It wouldn't matter how long you searched and how bright the light was outside; you would never find the keys.

Think of peace of mind as your lost keys. Where are you searching for them?

Happiness is what fuels success. Success can never bring you happiness.

Joy from the inside out is what leads to more creativity, endless motivation, and more productive work.

All the work we will do together will lead you here.

Leading you back home, to your own keys.

Today I choose to be my best self.

Sharing with you today my own morning insight that comes to me each day from Marianne Williamson. They don't always resonate and inspire me to share, but todays did. She was the one who inspired me to do this for this group, after I truly saw the importance of mornings in my work of choosing.

"Practice kindness and you start to become kind. Practice discipline and you start to become disciplined. Practice forgiveness and you start to become forgiving. Practice charity and you start to become charitable. Practice gentleness and you start to become gentle.

It doesn't matter whether you're in the mood to be gracious to the supermarket checkout person today; do it anyway - and watch how it begins to affect your mood. Choose the behaviour of the self you wish to be (your inner values - qualities you bring to how you want to treat yourself and others), and the synapses that make up that personality begin to form. Your best self already exists in the ethers, just waiting to be downloaded. We become gracious when we decide to be gracious. We have the power to generate as well as react to feelings; to hone our personalities as we travel through life. In the

words of George Elliot, "it's never too late to be what you might have been."

Today I choose to be my best self.

So is the power of belief. What you choose to believe is what you become.

For those who haven't met our **OWL**, she is here to guide you to your own inner wisdom very soon. She is a beautiful metaphor to help you make more heart centred choices that align with your values, rather than subconscious habitual ones.

O - to observe, to witness. What you're all doing.

W - willing. Willing to do what it takes, face your fears, sit in discomfort, confront your choices and be willing to make a different one that will take you towards the life you're wanting.

L - living your values. Your inner values are what will allow you to feel like you're inputting the coordinates to your inner GPS. Values can be hard to become conscious of because most of what we think we value isn't really ours. It's conditioned from outside of ourselves.

Values are the qualities we want to bring to how we treat ourselves (first and foremost), and others. Clarity with values comes when we ask ourselves how we would like others to describe us.

The Daily Insight

Our daily choices make up our lives.

Pretty sure that means we want to be choosing things daily that align with our own direction.

But so often, we're not.

We're reacting, we're repeating, we're wandering through each day like someone else is inputting the coordinates to our own GPS.

That never feels good.

And when I was living my life from this state, I was always exhausted trying to control everyone else around me to make myself feel better inside. Strange thing was I was totally unaware that that is what I was doing.

But living from this state of mind, coupled with a dysregulated nervous system, meant I had no choice on how I reacted to my emotional state.

We always have a choice. But we don't always see that we do.

Everything we do can be driven either by our subconscious mind - our past - or our conscious mind - our future. The work is to create awareness of the fact we always get to choose.

201

Choice is what gifts us with the ability to input the coordinates to our own GPS system, that will lead us down the path of our choosing how we treat ourselves and others around us.

It's the most important part of the work, that all you're noticing and observing is leading you towards.

The Daily Insight

Quiet courage - the type of courage needed to live a life aligned with your values.

It's incredible to know you have it within you, and it's always there waiting patiently for you to return. It can never be lost or destroyed.

It's one of those things you must just know is there. There's no randomised control trial that will confirm it for you.

You just must look for it, start to use it, and you will feel it. And this is your life safety net.

Your inbuilt security will always help you navigate any situation you're faced with. That will help you to use your values in your interactions with yourself and others, even when your mind or others want you to behave in another way.

It will feel like you're stepping out into an abyss when you start ignoring your mind and begin consciously listening to your heart. Don't expect it to feel any other way. It can't because your mind will be seeing and screaming danger is everywhere.

But there is no danger. That's all an illusion of your mind.

How can you start to feel this quiet courage more within you? By calling on it.

By consciously choosing your heart over your head. By creating space between your mind and body wanting you to instantly react. By choosing instead to wait to remember your values.

The work now is in getting clear on what matters to you deep in your heart. Then consciously aligning your behaviour with those qualities.

This is the path back home to you.

The Daily Insight

'Finding yourself' is not how it works.

You are not a ten-dollar bill lost in last winter's coat pocket. You are not lost.

Your true self is right there, buried under your thoughts born from cultural conditioning, other people's opinions, and inaccurate conclusions you drew as a child and adult that became your beliefs about who you are.

'Finding yourself' is actually a returning to yourself.

An unlearning, an excavation, a remembering of who you were before the world got its hands on you.

Are you ready for the magical inward journey?

Are you ready to step into the life you deserve to live?

Are you ready to see that you are everything you've been searching for?

Pick up your perfectly imperfect self and off you go.

Take me with you. I will walk beside you the entire time.

If you fall, brush yourself off and get back up.

It never matters how fast you travel, only that you do. Forgive yourself quickly, forgive others too.

If you forget like we all do, that's ok.

Gently remind yourself of your humanness and get back on the path. You only have this one beautiful life.

Embrace it all.

The End...

or I deeply hope for you, it has been a new beginning.

About the Author

Tracey is a holistic health and life coach from Melbourne, Australia. She is also a wife and a mum of 5.

She runs a successful coaching business helping people heal their bodies and minds. Prior to that she was a personal trainer for 12 years.

She herself has been through some major transformations in healing, from reversing prediabetes at age 40 to overcoming a lifetime of emotional eating and drinking habits. But far her biggest healing has come from an auto immune diagnosis, which saw her break free from co-dependency.

Tracey is also an author, a TEDx Speaker, a Master Coach within the Nutrition Network, and a podcaster. She also mentors other coaches

looking to truly show their clients where to look for long term healing and change.

You can connect with Tracey at her website: www.traceymcbeath.com.au

Printed in Great Britain
by Amazon

52534637R00121